06/17 5x L'I/17

RIBBONWORK

RIBBONWORK

25 decorative projects that celebrate the beauty of ribbons

CHRISTINE KINGDOM

Photography by Peter Williams

LORENZ BOOKS

This edition is published by Lorenz Books,
an imprint of Anness Publishing Ltd,
Blaby Road, Wigston,
Leicestershire LE18 4SE

info@anness.com

www.lorenzbooks.com; www.annesspublishing.com

If you like the images in this book and would
like to investigate using them for publishing,
promotions or advertising, please visit our website
www.practicalpictures.com for more information.

Publisher: Joanna Lorenz
Senior editor: Clare Nicholson
Photographer: Peter Williams
Designer: Peter Butler
Stylist: Georgina Rhodes
Illustrator: Lucinda Ganderton
Production Controller: Wendy Lawson

PUBLISHER'S NOTE
Although the advice and information in this book are
believed to be accurate and true at the time of going to
press, neither the authors nor the publisher can accept
any legal responsibility or liability for any errors or
omissions that may have been made nor for any
inaccuracies nor for any loss, harm or injury that comes
about from following instructions or advice in this book.

Bracketed terms are intended for American readers.

AUTHOR'S ACKNOWLDGEMENTS
I would like to thank Julie Watkins for her invaluable
help at every stage of copy preparation and checking;
Offray and Lion ribbon who kindly supplied the glorious
array of ribbons for both the photography and projects
in this book and whose generous support made the
whole thing possible; the Herbert Art Gallery and
Museum, Coventry, for their unique and beautiful
collection of ribbons and related literature; the team
at Anness Publishing, particularly Clare Nicholson;
Georgina Rhodes for the wonderful styling and Peter
Williams for the beautiful photography.
   I would also like to thank all the contributors whose
creative flair and enthusiasm keep ribboncrafts fresh and
exciting. And finally, my husband John and my sons
Richard and Nicky for their love and support.

3 9082 12727 2956

CONTENTS

INTRODUCTION

For centuries, ribbons have been used for decoration and as status symbols, tokens of love and badges of allegiance. As one of the cheapest and most widely available craft materials, they have lost none of their appeal. By mastering a few basic techniques, you can turn simple strands of colour into exquisite artefacts, or use them for gift wrapping, floristry and trimming costumes and furnishings. The 25 projects in this book provide a complete collection of wonderful items to make, and the gallery of work by contemporary designers gives further inspiration for creating your own beautiful ribbonwork.

Opposite: Today the choice of colours, fabrics, textures and styles of ribbons is wider than ever, ranging from traditional silks, satins and velvets to ultra-modern metallics and exotic prints.

The History of Ribbons

From the very earliest times, ribbons have served both practical and decorative purposes. From shoulder straps and belts to decorative borders, bows and rosettes, the use of ribbons has changed dramatically over time. The history of ribbons follows their development from individually woven symbols of status to the mass-produced selection available to everyone today, and offers a fascinating insight into the huge importance we attach to expression through clothing, for the history of ribbons is closely aligned to the history of fashion.

The earliest examples of ribbons – in the broad sense of narrow strips of fabric – are from ancient Egypt and can be dated to about 3000BC. It is impossible to say for certain how or where weaving was first discovered but, having produced lengths of fabric, people started draping them around their bodies and embellishing them in various ways.

In ancient Egypt, narrow tunics starting below the chest and extending to the ankles were often supported by a crossed shoulder strap, and sometimes narrow bands of fabric were drawn around the waist and fastened at the front to give more shape to the garment. The more elaborate the clothing, the higher the status of the wearer, and this pattern of dress continued through subsequent eras, including both the Greek and Roman civilizations.

During the Middle Ages, a wider variety of elaborate decorative borders began to be used to embellish clothing. In England, by the beginning of the 12th century, gowns had become relatively complex garments. The bodice was slit down either side from arm to hip and fitted with ribbons that were used to tie the material tightly across the upper part of the body. By the middle of the 12th century, skirts had become fuller with dozens of knife-pleats, and the tightness of the bodice was accentuated with a belt resembling a deep cummerbund, which was tied at the back with ribbons.

At the beginning of the 14th century, there began to be a clear differentiation between male and female costumes. Men's costumes became shorter, tunics being worn above the knee, while women's gowns remained long. Costumes for both sexes were tighter and more figure-revealing than ever before. Hairstyles and headdresses also underwent a considerable change during this period, paving the way for more formal devices for containing the hair.

Above: Late 19th-century night dressing-case. The formal fretwork border of velvet ribbon contains garlands of flowers worked in shaded silk ribbons and silk threads.

By the 16th century, trade with the New World had developed and a middle class emerged, eager to spend its wealth on imitating the style of the aristocracy. Henry VIII loved richly decorated garments and headdresses and, to protect himself and the Court from being copied, he introduced legislation preventing anyone but royalty and the aristocracy from wearing decorative embroidery, ribbons woven with gold and silver thread, brocades and jewellery. Shoes from this period were decorated with beautiful ribbon rosettes, while ladies entwined their hair or headdresses with ribbon. The rigidity and ostentation of late 16th-century costume are perfectly illustrated by Elizabeth I, whose gowns were almost entirely covered with pearls, embroidered motifs and bows.

The use of ribbons and other adornments was relatively modest during the Puritan period of the 17th century, but the restoration of the English monarchy in 1660 and the coming of age of France's Sun King, Louis XIV, in 1661 brought about a change of attitude in both countries. The Huguenots were forced to leave France in their thousands. In Holland and America, where they settled, their Puritan fashions survived, while the rest of Europe saw a period of extravagant ostentation. Louis XIV's powerful and dazzling court in France and the self-indulgent rule of Charles II in England were reflected in the costume of both men and women. Men's petticoat-breeches, doublets and shoes were invariably decorated all over with bunches of ribbon. Tight stockings were generally pulled over the breeches and fastened with a garter that was also decorated with a bunch of ribbons. Women's skirts were divided or drawn up with lavishly tied ribbon to reveal extremely ornate petticoats beneath.

The Court of Versailles dominated all matters of taste and fashion among the European aristocracy in the early 18th century. At the same time, the middle classes experienced increasing prosperity and for the first time fashion became the domain of the majority. Ribbons played an essential role, being used to trim gowns

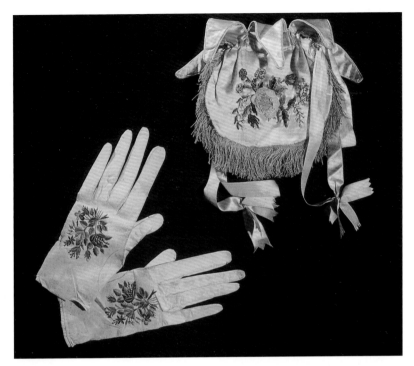

and bonnets, tie up hair for a ball, lace dainty shoes and in the form of waistbands, sashes, frills, favours and rosettes. Small children were smothered in ribbon, and curtains and cushions were embellished with broad bands of silk. Ribbons were produced in a dazzling variety of weaves and colours; plain, striped, checked, watered, shot, shaded and figured ribbons were all widely available.

England, with its technical and colonial advantages, saw tremendous advances in the textile industry. Coventry was at the centre of silk production and ribbon manufacturers prospered. They bought raw silk from France and Italy and delivered the finished product to London. An embargo on imported finished silk goods in 1766 ensured that Coventry had the monopoly for a considerable period.

Above: An embroidered satin drawstring bag and gloves from the early 19th century. Satin ribbons matching the bag have been used for the drawstrings.

In the early days of the trade, ribbon was woven on hand looms which produced one ribbon at a time. After 1770, the Dutch engine loom was introduced. Despite its name, it was still hand-operated but enabled the weaver to produce six ribbons simultaneously. During the Napoleonic wars, weavers were recruited for the army, leaving the trade short of labour, although the demand for ribbon was as high as ever. The smuggling of vast quantities of French ribbon almost became an industry in itself in coastal villages, and yet the demand was still not met.

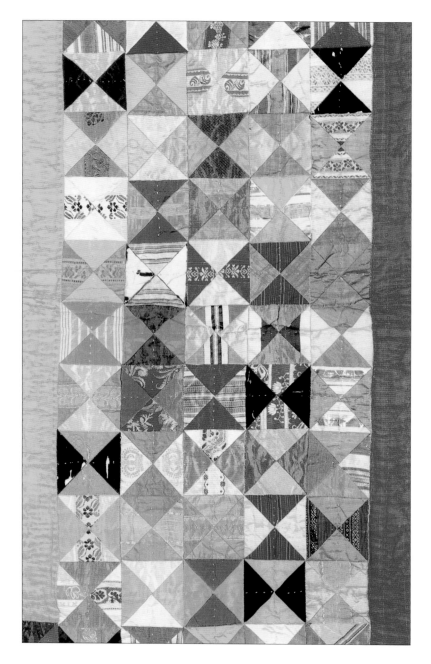

In 1813, a scalloped-edged ribbon became the rage and weavers had never known a time of such fierce demand for their product. In London, for a period of two years while the craze lasted, manufacturers could ask whatever prices they wished. However, at this time, the death of a member of the Royal Family would plunge the entire fashionable world into mourning. Black was the only acceptable trim for clothes and bonnets, and a whole season's production of coloured ribbons would become unmarketable. "I have determined to trim my lilac Sarsenet with black satin ribbon. Ribbon trimmings are all the fashion in Bath", wrote Jane Austen. Ribbon manufacturers always responded quickly to the trends of the day.

During the first half of the 19th century, the Industrial Revolution was in full swing and profit was a major concern. Wealth became more important than birth, and fashion was no longer dictated by nobility as it had been for centuries. Department stores sprang up in all major cities and off-the-peg clothes appeared for the first time. Two novel items became essential in a woman's wardrobe: the parasol and the large-brimmed hat. Both were extravagantly decorated with rosettes and bows. Handbags made their first appearance at the turn of the 19th century and were rapidly being made in every conceivable style and with all manner of ribbon embellishments.

In 1823, jacquard looms were introduced in Coventry, thus extending the variety of fancy ribbons available. Ribbon factories and mills were built, all making use of steam-powered looms, although workers using hand looms still

Left: A colourful patchwork quilt created from ribbons and silks. Made in England in the mid-18th century.

continued their trade, particularly in the countryside. By the middle of the 19th century, half the working population in the Coventry area was in the ribbon trade. The lifting of the trade embargo on foreign silk goods in 1824, resulted in fierce competition and French ribbons flooded into London stores. The increased prosperity of the time meant that working girls had a little money to indulge in a piece of ribbon to trim a hat, and Coventry found a new middle- and lower-class market.

Ribbons from Lyon and Saint-Etienne in France provided the main competition and were also the major influence on English manufacturers. The two towns produced an endless stream of novelties in silks, satins and velvets and, although ribbons of equal beauty were being produced in England, there was a certain prestige attached to the French collections. The French designs had always been copied or adapted by English manufacturers but it was around this time that English designers from

the newly established colleges of art and design in London were starting to produce ribbon patterns.

The period between 1850 and 1870 was one of unprecedented prosperity for an enormous number of people. Women's clothes became increasingly complex, made from two or three different materials and trimmed with a medley of folds, frills and pleats. Ribbons and braids were an integral part of the garments and by the 1880s, bustles became known as the 'upholstered style' because they were made from draperies more suited to furnishing a room than trimming a dress.

The turn of the 20th century saw a general softening of the silhouette and tucks, frills, ruchings and other ribbon trims were gradually modified. As the size and complexity of dresses diminished, hats grew larger and were trimmed with a profusion of ribbons and feathers. These extravagant hats gradually gave way to more modest creations: the cloche hat of the 1920s was quite plain but often trimmed with a fancy rosette on one side.

From the 1930s until quite recently, the significance of the ribbon as a fashion item diminished considerably, with just the occasional reappearance as trends dictated – during the flower power era of the 60s, for example. In more recent times, there has been a revival of interest in ribbons and ribboncrafts, although the emphasis is now on using them for home decoration rather than for adorning clothing. Ribbon embroidery is the new stitchcraft and ribbon weaving, pleating, plaiting and ruching are all being rediscovered and enjoyed.

Left: Handwoven silk taffeta produced by the Whitchurch silk mill, which is then cut into different widths for ribbons.

GALLERY

Ribbons are an extremley versatile medium, and presented here is a selection of some of the finest work by contemporary designers. Employing many different techniques, these craft artists have used ribbons for elaborate embellishments on hats, gloves and gowns, for complex weaving patterns, and as works of art in their own right. Once you have mastered the basic techniques used in the projects, these works of art will provide further ideas.

Left: RIBBON
SPIRAL HAT
This elegant ribbon hat was inspired by the natural way in which the ribbon spirals when pulled from the roll. Throughout her work, Jo Buckler likes to allow fabrics and materials to flow as their natural properties dictate. The spiralling organza ribbon was coiled around a straw hat with the gold edge of the organza ribbon forming an interesting herringbone effect. The ribbon is stitched at various points to secure in place.
Jo Buckler

Above: WAVES
WALL HANGING
The inspiration for this design came from the shapes that are created by weaving techniques used. Small-scale undulations are produced through the interaction of the bands of a thick wool weft and thin ribbon weft. Patricia Tindale

Opposite:
CHRISTENING
GOWN
Cream double-face satin ribbon has been appliquéd on to the gown using various simple techniques.
Jenny Banham

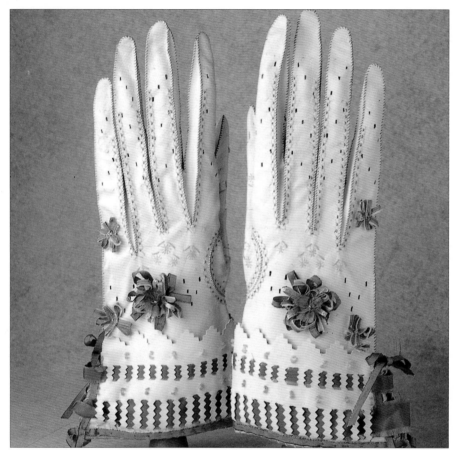

Below: RIBBON
INSTALLATION
*This work of art called
'impermanent -
impermanence' is
made from sheer and
opaque satin ribbons.
It was inspired by
city plans and grid
systems. As Roland
Barthes said 'The city
is an ideogram.'
Renata Brink*

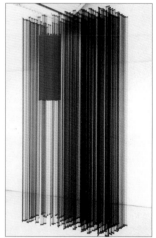

Above:
EMBROIDERED
GLOVES
*These hand-stitched
gloves, which are
embroidered with
ribbons, are based on
a 17th-century pair.
The decoration is
typical of the period
when ribbons were
used in profusion.
Pamela Woods*

Right:
KALEIDOSCOPE
*This puzzle is made of
90 wood-veneer
triangles, hot-glued to
nylon ribbon and
finished at each end
with magnetic catches.
The aim is to turn the
strip into a hexagon
and then 'flex' it to
exhibit the 15 different
patterns. Steve Cormack*

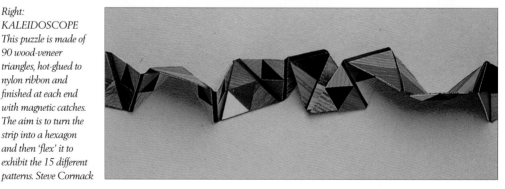

Right: RIBBON EMBROIDERY This beautiful embroidery was inspired by hydrangeas that Daphne Ashby saw on Jersey. It is composed mainly of machine embroidery with ribbon embellishment. First the bracts were drawn, outlined and shaded in. Then the tiny flowers were worked by hand using ribbon, beads and French knots. The foliage was machined without any further drawing on to the fabric. Daphne J. Ashby

Opposite: AFRICAN HANGING
This wall hanging was made by stitching together two layers of simple patchwork in a grid pattern. Selected areas of the patchwork are then cut away to reveal the layer underneath. The surface is covered with couched 'ribbons' of hand-dyed silk to create geometric patterns. Jenny Chippindale

Right: WOVEN CUSHION
The charm and beauty of this woven cushion lies in the fantastic colour scheme and texture of the velvet ribbons. Hikaru Noguchi

Above: INVITATION
This card was made by drawing a decorative border of delicate roses on to parchment paper. It was then colour-washed in watercolour before being decorated with ribbon rosebuds and bows. Lindsay Chalford Brown

Left: TREASURE CHEST
The lid of the chest is made up of a 15cm (6in) square of ribbon weaving worked in 3mm (⅛in) ribbons in shades of blue. It is enhanced with extra ribbons, held in place with single strands of metallic embroidery thread (floss), worked in cross stitch and French knots. The weaving was mounted on to a piece of card. Maureen Voisey

EQUIPMENT

Ribboncraft is an inexpensive hobby, requiring little outlay for tools and specialist equipment. Indeed, much of the equipment used to create the projects in the book will already be in the sewing basket or in everyday use around the home. Most ribbon projects involve some hand sewing, requiring needle, thread, dressmaker's pins and scissors. Listed below are the more unusual items you may need, but refer to the materials list for your chosen projects.

Bowmaker Many people find the hand-tied bow very tricky to master. This simple but ingenious wooden tool gives a professional finish every time. With a bowmaker you can make any number of consistently sized and shaped bows.

Imagine a Christmas tree bedecked with myriad bows, all beautifully tied, or a table for a special occasion trimmed with bows. The bowmaker can make bows of almost any size and takes a variety of ribbon widths from narrow up to the widest available. See supplier information at the back of the book for further details.

Glue guns are not essential but, as any craft worker who already uses one will know, they quickly become indispensable once purchased. They apply glue with speed and accuracy, even in tricky areas. There are various sizes in the two types available, hot- and cold-melt, so it is quite easy to select one to suit your needs and your budget. As with any adhesive product, it is important to keep glue guns out of children's reach.

Weaving board If you are going to undertake any ribbon-weaving or braiding projects, a weaving board is essential. Whether you buy or make one, it is important that the board is big enough to accommodate the whole weaving project. An ironing board can be used for weaving small pieces but would not be suitable for the Woven Ribbon Waistcoat project. A weaving board is a fabric-covered soft board that will take pins easily and securely. The weaving will be subjected

to a hot iron on completion so avoid using anything like polystyrene (Styrofoam), which will melt under such circumstances.

Wire and wire cutters Two types of florist's wire are used for making ribbon roses: stub (floral) wire and binding wire. It is important to use the two different weights as one is required to be flexible, the other to maintain stiffness (see Stemmed Ribbon Roses in the Basic Techniques section). Avoid using dressmaking scissors to cut florist's wire as they will soon be

Above: Specialist equipment, such as a glue gun, florist's tape (stem wrap) and stub (floral) wires, is required for a few of the projects in the book.

ruined beyond repair. Wire cutters or craft scissors are a worthwhile investment. Other floristry materials you may need include florist's tape (stem wrap) and artificial leaves. You can make your own leaves, following the technique described in the Stemmed Tartan Roses.

MATERIALS

Ribbons are a wonderful medium to work with as they come in such an amazing variety of textures, designs, colours and widths. There are ribbons for every occasion and every season, from baby pastels and frothy sheers to designer prints and brocades. As ribbon weaving keeps pace with modern technology, the choice becomes ever greater: woven-edge, wire-edge, satin, taffeta, colour-shaded, shot, grosgrain, gathered, pearled, metallic and iridescent ribbons are all readily available.

All the types of ribbon can be divided into two main categories: craft ribbon and washable, woven-edge ribbon.

Craft ribbons are purely decorative, designed and produced to be used for embellishment. Among craft ribbons, there are many interesting surface weaves and a variety of wired edgings. A satin stitched edge, often encasing a fine wire, is known as merrowed edging. Many craft ribbons are cut-edge ribbons, meaning that they have been specially treated to stiffen the fabric and prevent fraying, which is why they are so useful for crafts. Other ribbons fall into the craft category, even though they may not have wire edges, because they are not washable.

Woven-edge ribbons are narrow strips of fabric with selvages down either side. Many are made to very high standards to be used within the garment and soft-furnishing industries. Woven-edge ribbons are washable and each ribbon reel should carry full details of crease resistance and colour fastness, as well as washing instructions. If the reel does not carry this information, you should assume that the ribbon is not guaranteed in this manner.

Most ribbon widths are standard. The table overleaf will assist you in making any necessary conversions when purchasing ribbon but it is only a guideline. Ribbon is usually sold by the metre, the yard or in pre-cut packaged lengths. Embroidery ribbon can now be purchased in this way. The ribbon project will nearly always dictate whether you choose a woven-edge or craft ribbon. It will be clear whether or not the finished project will need cleaning and also the finished effect that is required. For example, a basic single-loop bow can be made from any type of ribbon and still look stunning, whereas a hand-tied bow will only give satisfactory results if wire-edge or soft, traditional ribbon is used. Do not feel restricted to using the ribbons listed in the project as there is a huge variety available today.

Ombré taffeta A finely woven taffeta with colour shading across the width. Variations include plaids and colour blends giving a lustrous finish and subtle tonal effects.

Grosgrain These ribbons have a distinctive crossways rib and are a stronger, denser weave than most other ribbon types. Grosgrains are make in solid colours, stripes, dots and prints. There are also satin and grosgrain combinations available.

Sheers These fine, almost transparent ribbons are available as plain ribbons or with satin, lurex or jacquard stripes. A thicker yarn is used along the selvage to give stability. This is known as a monofilament edge.

Jacquards An intricate pattern is incorporated in the weave. This can be multi- or mono-colour combinations, florals or geometric patterns which give a beautiful tapestry-like effect.

Wire-edge taffeta A fine weave with a matt rather than shiny finish. This product looks the same on both sides and is available plain or with lurex incorporated.

Weaves include plaids, checks and ombrés. Taffeta can also be printed or given a shimmering watermark finish. The wire-edge is usually encased so it is not visible.

Lace-edge Satins and jacquards are sometimes embellished with a lace edge. This is stitched or bonded onto the ribbon selvage and is particularly popular for bridal applications.

Shot-effect taffeta The use of different, often contrasting colours for the warp and weft results in a shot effect giving a really lustrous, colour-shaded finish, similar to shot silk. This product is available both wired and unwired.

Plaids and checks Popular classics, plaids and checks are usually taffeta weaves but are also often available in cut-edge ribbon.

Velvets The deep, plush pile of velvet is unmistakable and the depth of colour is exceptional. Cheaper imitation velvets are available.

Merrow-edge This describes the fine satin-stitched edge, usually incorporating a wire that is added to elaborate cut-edge ribbons for stability and decoration. It is often in lurex thread but can also be in a contrasting colour.

Moiré This effect is the result of a watermark finish applied during manufacture. It gives a lustrous finish.

Metallics These ribbons are made from or incorporate metallic or pearlized fibres. Many different weaves and finishes result in a number of combinations.

Cut-edge craft This type of ribbon is made from a wide fabric and then cut into strips. It is available wired or unwired and is only suitable for craft applications. The special finish stops the ribbon from fraying when it is cut into strips. These ribbons are not washable.

Satins Satins are either double-face (shiny on both sides) or single-face (shiny on one side and matt on the other). They are available in plain colours as well as printed. Some satin ribbons incorporate edgings such as picot- or feather-edge.

RIBBON CONVERSIONS	
1.5mm (¹⁄₁₆in)	36mm 1³⁄₈in)
3mm (¹⁄₈in)	39mm (1¹⁄₂in)
5mm (³⁄₁₆in)	50mm (2in)
7mm (¹⁄₄in)	56mm (2¹⁄₄in)
9mm (³⁄₈in)	67mm (2⁵⁄₈in)
12mm (¹⁄₂in)	70mm (2³⁄₄in)
15mm (⁵⁄₈in)	77mm (3in)
23mm (⁷⁄₈in)	80mm (3¹⁄₄in)
25mm (1in)	

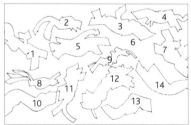

Key

1 Ombré taffeta ribbons	8 Plaid and check ribbons
2 Grosgrain ribbons	9 Velvet ribbons
3 Sheer ribbons	10 Merrow-edge
4 Jaquard ribbons	ribbons
5 Wire-edge taffeta ribbons	11 Moiré ribbons
6 Lace-edge ribbons	12 Metallic ribbons
7 Shot-effect taffeta ribbons	13 Cut-edge craft ribbons
	14 Satin ribbons

BASIC TECHNIQUES

Ribbons are a wonderfully versatile material to work with. They can be woven, braided, embroidered, appliquéd, or simply made into roses and bows. Of the many techniques commonly used in ribboncrafts, instructions are given in this chapter for those used to make the specific projects shown in the book.

RIBBON ROSES

Despite the finished look, roses are deceptively easy to make. There are several different techniques, employing various ribbon types, and each method will give a slightly different rose. The chart below gives the lengths of ribbon needed to make each type of rose depending on the width chosen. Experiment with different ribbon widths – the wider the ribbon, the larger the rose will be.

Ribbon Requirements

Use the chart below as a guide to ribbon requirements when making small ribbon roses (rosebuds) following any technique, or for larger stemmed and stitched roses. Allow an extra 10cm (4in) for all stemmed roses, for attaching the ribbon to the wire.

The quantities given are approximate and the fuller you wish to make the rose the more ribbon you will use. The type of ribbon will determine the look of the rose. For example, roses made from satin ribbon will almost certainly be more delicate and less full than those made from wire-edge taffeta.

Wire-edged Ribbon Rose

This quick and easy ribbon rose is perfect for a variety of crafts, for trimming gifts or special-occasion clothing and accessories such as bridal wear. A wire stem is easily added, making the rose suitable for attachment to hairslides (barrettes), hairbands, headbands or for wearing in a buttonhole.

You Will Need

Wire-edge ribbon, 90cm x 39mm
  (1yd x 1½in)
Needle and matching thread
Stub (floral) wire, 20cm (8in) (optional)
Florist's tape (stem wrap) (optional)
Artificial leaves (optional)

1 Tie a knot in one end of the wire-edge ribbon. From the other end, carefully start pulling the wire from one edge of the ribbon, causing the ribbon to gather.

2 Hold the knot like a stem and ease the gathered edge around it to form a rose. Use the wire strand that is now exposed to secure the raw end to the base of the rose. One or two stitches may be required.

Ribbon Width	Ribbon Length	
	Rosebuds	Stitched/Stemmed Roses
5mm (³⁄₁₆in)	7.5cm (3in)	13cm (5in)
7mm (¼in)	7.5cm (3in)	20cm (8in)
9mm (³⁄₈in)	7.5cm (3in)	20cm (8in)
15mm (⁵⁄₈in)	15cm (6in)	40cm (16in)
23mm (⁷⁄₈in)	15cm (6in)	50cm (20in)
39mm (1½in)	60cm (24in)	1m (40in)
56mm (2¼in)	80cm (32in)	1.5m (1²⁄₃yd)
Ribbon less than 15mm (⁵⁄₈in) wide is not recommended for stemmed roses		

3 Gently tease the ungathered edge into the shape of rose petals.

4 If you wish to add a stem to the rose, do this before finishing off the raw end in step two. Take a length of stub wire and twist one end very gently around the stem of the rose to secure it. Wrap the exposed wire strand from the ribbon around the wire stem.

5 Wrap the stem with florist's tape, binding on artificial leaves as you work. The adhesive tape will help to keep the stem firmly attached to the rose.

Stitched Ribbon Rose

The highly decorative stitched rose is perfect for adorning a hat, a ballgown, soft furnishings or fashion accessories. Use singly or in groups for thoroughly romantic appeal. The ombré taffeta ribbon used here has a gorgeous two-tone effect and there are many more wonderful colour combinations to choose from.

A stem and artificial florist's leaves can be added to the rose when required for accessories such as a corsage, headdress or bouquet. Follow the technique for the Stemmed Ribbon Rose and, as a general rule, use a heavy gauge wire for the stem, ensuring that it is flexible enough to be looped and twisted. A finer gauge is used for binding the rose. Whatever the wire, be sure to use craft scissors or wire cutters to cut it.

You Will Need
Ribbon (see chart on page 22)
Needle and matching thread
Dressmaker's pins

1 Fold down one end of the ribbon at a right angle and so that it extends below the edge of the remaining ribbon by about 2.5cm (1in). Stitch through both layers to secure. This provides a working handle. Working from left to right, coil the ribbon into a tube, turning about six times. Make a couple of stitches at the base to secure the rose centre.

2 To make each petal, fold the ribbon to the outside at a right angle, about 2.5cm (1in) from the rose centre, so that the loose end hangs down vertically. Place a pin in the fold and turn the bud loosely into the fold, until the ribbon again runs horizontal. Secure the petal with a stitch and remove the pin. The stitching point will be higher than before, as the bud and twisted fold are almost level.

3 Continue making folds and stitching until there is about 7.5cm (3in) of ribbon remaining. Fold again and stitch the raw edge to the base of the rose, making small pleats as necessary. The completed roses can be stitched or glued in place, as appropriate. Stitched roses can be carefully laundered, providing the ribbon selected is washable and crease resistant.

Stemmed Ribbon Rose

Stemmed ribbon roses are made using the same technique as stitched roses but are formed around a wire stem. A stemmed rose requires about 10cm (4in) more ribbon than a stitched rose. Stemmed roses can be made using various ribbon widths and with a tight or loose tension to produce rosebuds and roses of different sizes, as you would find in a natural bouquet. Ribbons narrower than 15mm (⅝in) are too fiddly to work with for stemmed roses. The Stemmed Tartan Rose project is a perfect example of a loosely woven ribbon rose and demonstrates an unusual and witty application for tartan ribbon. People who prefer to use a needle and thread rather than binding wire should follow the Stemmed Tartan Rose steps rather than the instructions given below.

You Will Need:

Stub (floral) Wire, 20–30cm (8–12in)
Florist's stub wire, 50cm (20in)
Ribbon (see chart on page 22)
Florist's tape (stem wrap), 20cm (8in)
Artificial rose leaves
Wire cutters

1 Make a hook at one end of the stub wire. Thread the binding wire through the loop, twisting several times to hold it securely.

2 Fold one end of the ribbon over the loop top, then bind at the base with the binding wire.

3 Make the rose centre by twisting the ribbon around the loop several times. Bind at the base.

4 Using the stitched rose technique, fold the ribbon to the outside at a right angle and turn the rose into the fold to form a petal.

5 Bind the ribbon to hold the petal in place before you continue making more petals. Continue making petals until you have the required size.

6 Fold the raw edge to the base and bind securely. Cut off any excess binding wire.

7 Twist the florist's tape around the stem, starting as high as possible to conceal all the wire. Bind in the artificial leaves as you work down the stem.

RIBBON WEAVING

Weaving ribbons is an immensely satisfying craft and it produces some dazzling effects, as can be seen in the Basket-weave Cushion and Woven Ribbon Waistcoat projects.

Ribbon weaving can be used for many different soft furnishings, such as cushions, bolsters, bedspreads and wall hangings. On a smaller scale, it can be used in panels on bridal gowns, christening robes and evening wear. Festive tree hangings, potpourri sachets, pin cushions and table mats are all suitable projects for ribbon weaving. Simple woven squares or hearts can be appliquéd on to patchwork, trinket boxes or hat boxes.

The weaving methods described here are all fused on to iron-on interfacing. Other techniques require the ribbon to be stitched (see the Basket-weave Cushion project). Any type of ribbon can be used for weaving, providing that colour fastness or laundering are not a consideration. If these factors are important, then you should work with washable, woven-edge ribbons.

The ribbon weaving technique is reversed when working with velvet ribbon. In order to protect the velvet pile, the ribbon should be placed face down on the weaving board and woven with the wrong side facing you. When complete, place the interfacing square, adhesive side down, on to the back of the velvet ribbon and fuse in place.

Little equipment is required for weaving but the following items are essential: Felt-tipped pen • Ruler and tape measure • Weaving board large enough to accommodate the finished piece of weaving • Glass-headed dressmaking pins • Scissors • Steam iron or dry iron with damp cloth

Ribbon Requirements

Ribbon requirements will vary depending on the ribbon width, type of weave and area to be covered. Any diagonal weave such as the tumbling blocks weave will require more ribbon than others. As with knitting, requirements will also depend on the weaver's tension: a loose tension will probably require a little more ribbon than is stated in the chart below.

Basic Steps For Weaving

1 Cut out a square of iron-on interfacing the size of the weaving area. Mark the outside boundary to include an ample seam allowance as a guide during weaving. You will weave up to or just beyond this point. Pin the interfacing to the board, ensuring the glue side is facing up.

2 Start the weaving by pinning the ends of the warp (vertical) ribbons in place along the top edge of the interfacing. Do not pin the bottom edge. Start weaving the weft (horizontal) ribbons. Pin each ribbon at both ends. Always angle the pins away from the weaving as you will benefit from the extra space when pressing later. When the weaving is complete, the bottom edge of warp ribbons may be pinned before pressing.

RIBBON QUANTITIES FOR WOVEN SQUARES

The quantities given are for the whole square. If using two or more colours, divide the quantity by that number. All measurements include a 2.5cm (1in) seam allowance.

RIBBON WIDTH	RIBBON LENGTH		
	10 x 10CM (4 x 4IN) SQUARE	20 x 20CM (8 x 8IN) SQUARE	30 x 30CM (12 x 12IN) SQUARE
5mm ($^3/_{16}$in)	6m (6$^1/_2$yd)	20m (22yd)	42m (46yd)
7mm ($^1/_4$in)	4.2m (4$^1/_2$yd)	14.6m (16yd)	30.2m (33 yd)
9mm ($^3/_8$in)	3.4m (3$^3/_4$yd)	11m (12yd)	23.2m (25yd)
15mm ($^5/_8$in)	2.2m (2$^1/_2$yd)	6.6m (7$^1/_4$yd)	14m (15$^1/_4$yd)
23mm ($^7/_8$in)	1.4m (1$^1/_2$yd)	4.6m (5yd)	9.2m (10yd)

3 When the weaving is complete, fuse the ribbons to the interfacing using a moderate dry iron. Press the ribbons at the outer edge using the tip of the iron.

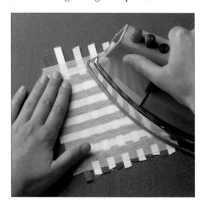

4 When the ribbons are firmly fixed, remove all the pins. Turn to the wrong side and press again with a steam iron. Leave to cool before proceeding with the project.

Plain Weave

You Will Need:
For a 30cm (12in) Square:
Lightweight iron-on interfacing,
    35.5 x 35.5cm (14 x 14in)
Pale ribbon, 15.1m x 7mm (16½yd x ¼in)
Dark ribbon, 15.1m x 7mm (16½yd x ¼in)

1 Mark a 2.5cm (1in) seam allowance all around the square of interfacing and pin it to the weaving board glue side up. Cut the warp ribbon into 35.5cm (14in) lengths. Pin the ends to the top edge of the interfacing. Butt the ribbons edge to edge, not overlapping.

2 Cut the weft ribbon into 35.5cm (14in) lengths and start weaving horizontally from the lefthand side. Weave the first weft ribbon over the first warp, under the second, then over and under to the end. Push the ribbon up to the top seam line and pin it at either end, placing the pins at the extreme side of the seam line and making sure the ribbon is taut.

3 Weave the second weft ribbon under the first warp and over the second, then under and over to the end. Alternate the weaving of the weft ribbons in this way until the whole of the weaving area is covered.

4 Check that the ribbons are all positioned before pressing, as detailed in steps 3 and 4 of Basic Steps for Weaving. If the last weft ribbon overlaps the bottom seam line by more than 9mm (⅜in), push the weft ribbons closer or remove the last ribbon.

Patchwork Weave

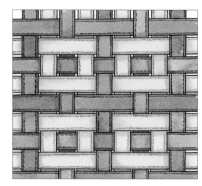

This weave is worked in three colours (A, B and C). Colour C will form the 'bull's eye' centre and is the brightest colour. Here it is the red ribbon. Colour A (light blue) defines the 'patchwork square' and should be bold enough to create some definition. Yellow provides the third colour (B) for this patchwork weave.

You Will Need:
For a 30cm (12in) Square:
Lightweight iron-on interfacing,
    35.5 x 35.5cm (14 x 14in)
Ribbon A, 8.5m x 9½mm (13¼yd x ⅜in)
Ribbon B, 12m x 9mm (13¼yd x ⅜in)
Ribbon C, 5.5m x 9mm (6yd x ⅜in)

1 Prepare the interfacing as detailed in Basic Steps for Weaving and cut all the ribbons into 35.5cm (14in) lengths.

2 Pin the ends of the warp ribbons to the top edge of the iron-on interfacing following the sequence ABCB to the end.

(Extra sequences may be added, providing they are added equally to either side of the weave.)

3 Starting in the top lefthand corner of the interfacing, pin the ends of the weft ribbons down the side of the interfacing in the sequence ABCD to the end. Weave the weft ribbons in the following sequence:
Row 1: over AB, under C, then over BAB, under C to the end (weaving over all the ribbons except C).
Row 2: under A, over BCB to the end (weaving over all the ribbons except A).
Row 3: over A, under B, over C, under B to the end (weaving over A and C ribbons).
Row 4: as row 2.

4 Bond the ribbons to the interfacing as detailed in Basic Steps for Weaving.

Zigzag Weave

This weave is most effective in two colours. Subtle or bold colours will give different looks. You can vary the ribbon widths.

You Will Need:
For a 30cm (12in) Square:
Lightweight iron-on interfacing, 35.5 x 35.5cm (14 x 14in)
Pale ribbon, 15.4m x 7mm (16¾yd x ¼in)
Dark ribbon, 14.6m x 7mm (16yd x ¼in)

1 Prepare the interfacing and ribbons as detailed in Basic Steps for Weaving. Alternating the pale and dark colours, pin the ends of the warp ribbons to the top edge of the interfacing.

2 Pin the ends of the weft ribbons down the lefthand side of the interfacing, alternating the pale and dark colours. Weave the weft ribbons in the following sequence of four rows:
Row 1: pale ribbon under two, over two to the end.
Row 2: dark ribbon under one, over two, under two, over two to the end.
Row 3: pale ribbon over two, under two to the end.
Row 4: dark ribbon over one, under two, over two, under two to the end.

3 Bond the ribbons to the interfacing as detailed in Basic Steps for Weaving.

Tumbling Blocks Weave

A favourite patchwork and quilting pattern in the 19th century, this three-dimensional weave employs three colours, usually a medium, a dark and a pale tone. The effect of the optical illusion can be very striking or quite subtle, depending on the choice of ribbon type and colour. Tumbling blocks weave is worked in two stages:

the basic warp and weft ribbons are woven first, then a narrower ribbon is woven diagonally through them.

You Will Need:
For a 30cm (12in) Square:
Lightweight iron-on interfacing, 35.5 x 35.5cm (14 x 14in)
Warp ribbon, 11.7m x 9mm (12¾yd x ⅜in)
Weft ribbon, 11.7m x 9mm (12¾yd x ⅜in)
Diagonal ribbon, 14.6m x 7mm (16yd x ¼in)

1 Prepare the interfacing as detailed in Basic Steps for Weaving. Cut the warp and weft ribbons into 35.5cm (14in) lengths. There should be 33 lengths in each colour ribbon.

2 Pin the ends of the warp ribbons to the top edge of the interfacing and pin the ends of the weft ribbons down the lefthand side of the interfacing. Ensure the ribbons lie edge to edge, not overlapping. Weave the weft ribbons in the following sequence of three rows:
Row 1: over one, under one, then over two, under one to the end.
Row 2: under one, over two to the end.
Row 3: over two, under one to the end.

3 Use the diagonal ribbon in one complete length with a safety pin in the lead end. Start weaving from the bottom righthand corner. Weave in the sequence over two weft ribbons, under two warp, up to the top lefthand corner. Check the weave, then pin the ends and cut the ribbon. Weave the next diagonal above the first and fill in this area before weaving the area below the first diagonal. You may have to remove pins as you weave. Always replace them before going on to the next diagonal.

4 Bond the ribbons to the interfacing as detailed in Basic Steps for Weaving.

Plain Weave

Bows are probably the first thing that come to mind when thinking about ribbon. There are several ways of tying a bow, be it large and floaty or small and dainty, and all are fairly easy to accomplish. If you are all fingers and thumbs when it comes to tying ribbon, try using a bowmaker (see Equipment and Suppliers sections). The different parts of a bow are known as the loop, neck and tail.

Diagram

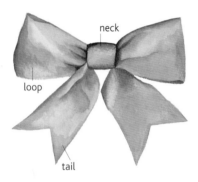

Satin ribbon is often a first choice for bows, but do not overlook novelty ribbons such as prints and lurex. Sheers make luxurious bows for gift wrapping. Experiment with different colours and widths, working the ribbons in layers or making separate bows and then layering them for a tiered effect. As a general rule, if the ribbon can be tied in a tight knot, it is suitable for hand-tying or can be used in a bowmaker. If the ribbon is too stiff, it will need to be pleated and stitched or bound with binding wire in the centre. The stitching or wire is easily concealed by gluing a strip of ribbon in place.

The tails are as important to a bow's appearance as the loops. They need to be in proportion to the loops. Leave the tails as long as possible until you are sure

about the required length. Cut the ends diagonally or in a chevron (an inverted 'V'). This not only looks attractive but also prevents a woven ribbon from fraying.

Make sure you have enough ribbon to make the bow; they often take more ribbon than expected, as you need to allow ease in the loop. Generally, bows made on a bowmaker are easier to manipulate, leaving your hands free to fashion the tails and keeping the right side facing out. There is less control with a hand-tied bow but you can always put a few stitches at the back of the bow once it is tied to help stabilize the centre and maintain the loop and tail positions.

For the following bows you will need: Ribbon • Florist's wire • Craft scissors • Glue gun • Needle and matching thread

Hand-tied Bow

The Gift Boxes project includes several ideas for gift wrapping using simple boxes and bows. The classic hand-tied bow is fashioned from one continuous strip of ribbon and requires no stitching or gluing. Everyone has made one of these bows at one time or another.

Place a length of ribbon on the work surface, and bring both ends into the middle so that they overlap. Pick up a loop in each hand – you now have two loops and two tails. Make any adjustments to the loop and tail size. Fold the left loop over the right, round to the back and through the centre hole. Pull the centre tight, adjusting to make loops and tails of equal size.

As a variation on the hand-tied bow, the neck of the bow can be secured with wire or ribbon (see diagram).

This bow can be made from wire-edge or traditional soft ribbon for gift-wrapping or embellishing craft projects and garment trimming.

1 Fold each half of the ribbon across the centre to make two loops and tails. Hold the ribbon securely at the neck.

2 Bind a piece of wire tightly around the neck of the bow.

3 Conceal the wire by wrapping a small piece of matching or contrasting ribbon around the neck of the bow. Secure it with glue or a couple of small handstitches at the back.

4 Gently pull the bow loops and trimmed tails into the desired shape.

Double-loop or Multi-loop Bow

These attractive bows can be made from any type of ribbon and are formed from a single length.

1 Fold the ribbon length into the desired number of loops.

2 Find the mid-point of the folded loops and form the neck of the bow by binding with a piece of wire or stitching.

3 Conceal the wire or stitching by wrapping a small piece of ribbon around the neck. Secure it with glue or a couple of stitches at the back.

Pompom Bow

This very extravagant, frothy bow is best suited to cut-edge craft ribbons and narrow sheers. Woven-edge ribbons such as satins will not work for this bow which is made from a series of loops secured with wire. Allow about 2m (2¼yd) of ribbon for an average bow, less for small pompons and more for large.

1 Start with a loop of ribbon that is equal to the required diameter of the finished bow. Wrap the ribbons around the length of this first loop about ten times or until all the ribbon is used up. Flatten the loops to form a rectangle. Taking care not to cut too close to the centre, cut the corners diagonally, as shown in the picture above.

2 Bring the cut corners together to meet in the middle, forming the neck of the bow. Wrap a short length of wire around the neck.

3 Pull out the loops, twisting them in different directions.

4 Trim the ribbon ends diagonally or in a chevron, as shown here.

RIBBON EMBROIDERY

Ribbon embroidery is exactly the same as any other embroidery, the only difference being that the stitches are worked with ribbon. The texture and width of the ribbon produces raised embroidery and the amazing range of shades available means that very life-like results can be achieved.

The real secret of successful ribbon embroidery is to remember that you are trying to recreate the look and feel of the subject, be it daisies, roses or tulips.

Tips for Ribbon Embroidery

To thread the needle, pass the end of the ribbon through the eye of the needle. Then push the point of the needle through the same end of the ribbon and pull. As with other types of embroidery, it is best to work with an embroidery hoop. Do not let the ribbon twist too much or it will knot. Knots can be undone easily as long as they have not been pulled too tightly. Try to weave in the ribbon ends at the back of the embroidery. They seldom come through but they might show through to the front.

Running Stitch

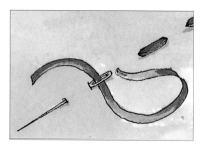

Pass the needle regularly in and out of the fabric to create the line of stitching. Keep the stitches small and evenly spaced on both the front and back of the work. Use your finger or a large needle to prevent the ribbon from twisting.

French Knots

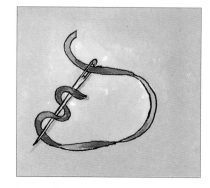

1 Bring the needle up through the fabric to the right side. Hold the ribbon taut with one hand and twist the needle around the ribbon twice.

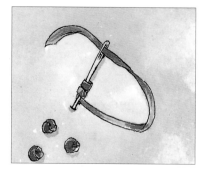

2 Still holding the ribbon, neaten the twists, then turn the needle to go back down through the fabric at almost the same spot it came up. The needle and ribbon should go through the twists. Ribbon French knots are easier if they are completed one at a time, rather than taking the needle straight back through for the next knot.

Spider's Web Rose

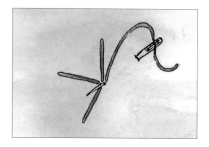

1 Bring the needle up through the fabric to the right side. Hold the ribbon taut with one hand and twist the needle around the ribbon twice.

2 Bring the ribbon up through the centre of this circle of spokes and start weaving in and out of the spokes in a spiral. Let the ribbon twist naturally as you form the rose.

3 Pass the needle under the rose and back down through the fabric.

Lazy Stitch or Detatched Chain

1 Bring the ribbon up through the fabric. Push the needle back down again at almost the same spot, leaving a loop of ribbon. Come back up through the fabric inside the loop and pull gently.

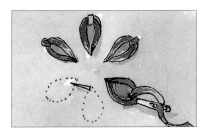

2 Take the needle back down again, over the loop to secure it in place. Bring the needle up at the central tip of the next petal.

Chain Stitch

Loop the ribbon under the needle's tip. Hold the ribbon down as you draw the needle through the fabric. Push the needle back through the hole it left to form the next stitch.

Blanket Stitch

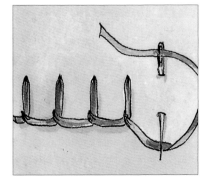

Work a line of vertical stitches and, as you draw the needle through the fabric, catch the ribbon under the needle's tip. Pull the ribbon through then insert the needle into the fabric parallel to the previous stitch.

Cross Stitch

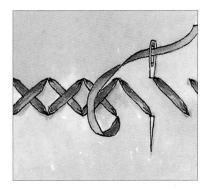

Cross stitch is worked in two parts and the top stitches should always lie in the same direction, usually from bottom left to top right. Work a row of diagonal stitches from right to left, then complete the crosses with a second row of diagonal stitches worked in the opposite direction.

Back Stitch

Back stitch produces an unbroken line of stitching suitable for outlining designs. First make a small stitch and pull the needle through the fabric. Insert the needle into the hole at the end of the previous stitch, then bring it up through the fabric a stitch length further on and repeat.

Slip Stitch

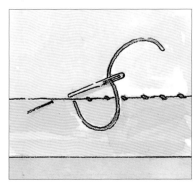

Slip stitch should be nearly invisible. Pick up two threads of the single fabric and slip the needle through the fold for about 5mm (³⁄₁₆in). Draw the needle through to make a tiny stitch.

SHELL APPLIQUÉD BAG

At last, a practical use for the beachcomber's booty! Display that collection of pretty shells, gathered over the years, by attaching them to a bag with ribbons. Use the bag for your future beachcombing excursions or as a furnishing accessory in the conservatory (sunroom) or the bathroom. Purchased shells can be substituted or, for an entirely different look, rummage through the button box for those beautiful button oddments that are far too pretty to throw away. Use a ribbon width to fit the size of the buttonholes. Trim the handles with ribbons too.

1 Arrange the shells on the bag and secure in place with masking tape.

2 Thread the needle with ribbon and tie a double knot at one end. Remove the tape from one shell. Secure the shell with a cross stitch (see Basic Techniques). Knot the ribbon on the inside of the bag.

3 Attach long shells with two cross stitches or by lacing the ribbon over one end of the shells. Fasten the ribbon securely inside the bag. Continue until all the shells are attached to the bag.

4 For the finishing touch, decorate the straps of the bag with ribbon. Thread the needle with ribbon and tie a double knot at one end. Starting with the knot on the outside of the strap, work a row of running stitches along one edge. Finish with a double knot on the outside of the strap. Decorate the other edges of each strap in the same way, using a different colour of ribbon.

Materials and Equipment You Will Need
Hessian (burlap) beach bag • Shells, some with drilled holes • Masking tape • Embroidery ribbon in 'seaside' colours, 5mm (³/₁₆in) •
Crewel needle • Scissors

COUNTRY LAMPSHADE

The simplicity of this project beautifully illustrates the old adage, 'less is more'. The addition of ribbon to this ordinary lampshade transforms the piece into a designer accessory, without the designer price tag! To calculate the amount of ribbon required for lacing, measure around the top and the bottom of the shade, add the two measurements together and multiply this figure by two and a half. This is a good project for the beginner.

1 If the lampshade is already laced on to the frame, remove the lacing and lace with 9mm (⅜in) cream matt ribbon. If not previously laced, punch evenly spaced holes around the top and bottom edges. Secure the ribbon lacing with a knot inside the lampshade.

2 Cut short pieces of cream matt ribbon in lengths ranging from 4.5 to 7cm (1¾ to 2¾in). Fray the ends.

4 Alternate the cross stitches with running stitches to secure the ribbon pieces. Apply the ribbons at random all over the shade.

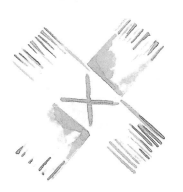

3 Thread the needle with a double length of embroidery thread. Hold the ribbon pieces against the lampshade either singly or in pairs, overlapping crossways. Secure in place with one or two cross stitches (see Basic Techniques).

Materials and Equipment You Will Need
Paper lampshade • Tape measure • Cream matt ribbon, 9mm (⅜in) • Hole punch • Scissors • Cream matt ribbons in various widths • Crewel needle • Cream cotton perle embroidery thread (floss)

TABLE SETTING

Trimming is the main function of ribbons. Here a plain table mat is transformed to match a dinner service or simply to brighten an otherwise purely functional item. Whenever you apply ribbons, always consider their intended use, the setting in which they will be utilized and, of course, laundry requirements. Extend the embellishment to cloth napkin rings and table linen too. A pure white tablecloth can be trimmed with rich gold ribbons for understated dining elegance. Co-ordinate table linen for a wedding breakfast to complement the bridal colours. The possibilities are there for you to explore.

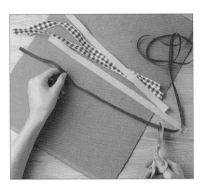

1 Calculate ribbon requirements by measuring all around the edges of the table mat, adding 20cm (8in) for turnings. Cut each colour of ribbon into four lengths, one for each edge of the mat plus a 2.5cm (1in) turning allowance at each end.

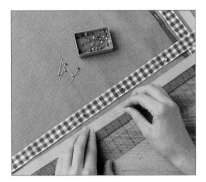

2 Starting from the outside edge, lay the ribbons in place. Use the ruler to ensure the ribbons are parallel to the edge and pin in place, leaving the ends free.

4 Sew the ribbons down using an invisible slip stitch along each edge, working the stitches closely together (see Basic Techniques). Turn under the raw ends and sew to the back of the table mat. Press the piece under a damp cloth.

3 Interlace the ribbons to produce a woven effect where they overlap at the corners and pin in place. Tack (baste) with contrasting thread and remove the pins.

Materials and Equipment You Will Need

Woven table mats • Ruler • Contrasting grosgrain ribbon, 9mm (⅜in) • Contrasting checked ribbon, 25mm (1in) • Toning grosgrain ribbon, 15mm (⅝in) • Scissors • Dressmaker's pins • Needle and contrasting and matching threads • Iron and damp cloth

WOVEN FOLDER

School projects or a college thesis often deserve much more than an ordinary, store-bought folder to preserve and protect them. This beautiful woven ribbon folder is sure to enhance the contents. The clever use of the heraldic fleur-de-lis ribbon and its plain burgundy reverse face guarantees full marks for this folder! Materials used to make the folder such as the book cloth and artist's lining paper should be readily available from suppliers of artist's or craft materials.

1 Line the two boards with black paper, gluing in place. To make the gusset of the folder, cut an 85.5 x 10cm (33½ x 4in) strip of book cloth or stiffened cloth and line it with artist's black paper. Fold the strip in half along the length, then fold the two halves in half again to create a concertina effect.

2 Mark a point 27cm (10½in) from each end of the strip. Fold the strip lengthways at the first point so that you have a double layer. Carefully cut a triangle out of each corner. Open out, then fold and cut the strip at the other 27cm (10½in) point in the same way.

3 Fold the strip at the two 27cm (10½in) points so that the two end sections of the gusset strip are at right angles to the middle section.

▶

Materials and Equipment You Will Need
Two pieces of stiff board, 35.5 x 25cm (14 x 10in) • Sheet of artist's black lining paper • PVA (white) glue • Glue spreader or paintbrush • Book cloth or stiffened fabric, 1m x 50cm (40 x 20in) • Pencil • Ruler • Scissors • Chisel • Hammer • Piece of wood • Black ribbon, 90cm x 7mm (1yd x ¼in) • Iron-on interfacing, 35.5 x 23cm (14 x 9in) • Masking tape • Burgundy fleur-de-lis ribbon, 4.6m x 39mm (5yd x 1½in) • Iron

4 Glue the two boards inside the gusset so that their edges lie inside the two outermost folds on the gusset strip. Press all the folds and creases firmly. Cut two pieces of book cloth slightly narrower than the boards but 5cm (2in) longer. Stick these to the outside of the boards, leaving the excess at the open edge to be turned over later.

6 Tape the interfacing to a weaving board, glue side up. Cut the fleur-de-lis ribbon into eight 27cm (10½in) strips and six 40cm (16in) strips. Place the eight shorter ribbons side by side over the interfacing and hold them in place with masking tape.

8 Trim the edges of the weaving, leaving a 2cm (¾in) allowance. Fold this allowance over the interfacing and iron carefully. Glue down the edges if this is necessary.

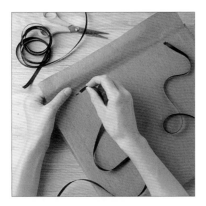

5 Chisel two holes into each side of the top edge of the folder. Protect the boards while you do this by placing a piece of wood between them. Cut the 7mm (¼in) ribbon into four lengths and thread one through each hole. Turn over the excess lining and glue down to secure the ribbons inside the folder.

7 Weave the six longer ribbons, plain side up, through the fleur-de-lis ribbons, following the plain-weave technique (see Basic Techniques). Make sure the weaving is even and tight. Press with a dry moderate iron when complete to fuse the ribbon to the interfacing.

9 Glue the woven panel to the front of the folder to complete.

SUNFLOWER JACKET

Customize clothing with a colourful piece of ribbon appliqué. The beauty of ribbon appliqué lies in the woven edges, which require no fiddly hemming. Tricky curves and angles are easy to work. The sunflower is a nice bright motif for a child's denim jacket, while animal motifs would make a fun alternative. More sophisticated designs can be appliquéd to add glamour to plain evening wear. Sheer ribbons, metallics, silks and taffetas would all be suitable for such a project. Keep the idea in mind as a way of covering up holes or stains on a favourite shirt or sweater.

1 Mark the design area on the jacket as a rough guide for the appliqué work. Start the appliqué by stitching the end of the brown ribbon to the centre of the design area. Sew the ribbon in a spiral, overlapping the coils and turning the ribbon over itself to form the coils. Sew along the inside edge of the ribbon as you make the spiral, using back stitch or running stitch to secure the outer edge of the previous coil (see Basic Techniques). Leave the outer edge of the completed spiral unsewn.

2 Cut 11 flower-petal shapes from the yellow ribbon. To make the ribbon easier to work with, cut only the tip of the petal, not the edges; this will prevent the edges from fraying. If you want to make the petal thinner, you can turn the edges under when you sew the petals down.

3 Start stitching the petals around the brown flower centre, turning under the raw edges and tucking the base of each petal under the unsewn edge of the flower centre.

Materials and Equipment You Will Need

Jacket or other garment • Dressmaker's marking pen or pencil • Brown double-face satin ribbon, 1.5m x 12mm (1²/₃yd x ¹/₂in) • Needle and matching threads • Yellow double-face satin ribbon, 1m x 39mm (40 x 1¹/₂in) • Scissors • Leaf-green double-face satin ribbon, 50cm x 39mm (40 x 1¹/₂in) • Embroidery threads (flosses)

4 Continue adding petals around the centre, overlapping some of the edges. Leave a gap at the bottom for the last two flower petals to be added after the flower stem.

5 Cut the flower stem from the leaf-green ribbon. Tuck the top end under the outer edge of the flower centre and sew the stem in place, using green embroidery thread. Turn under the bottom raw edge before stitching. Sew the last two petals over the stem.

7 Decorate the flower centre with small French knots, working in brown embroidery thread. Stitch one on top of the other if you wish, to give a more textured appearance.

6 Sew around the outer edge of the flower centre, securing all the flower petals and the top of the stem.

8 To finish off, cut two leaves from the green ribbon and stitch to either side of the stem. Stitch veins on the leaves using a small running stitch and some green embroidery thread.

RIBBON PICTURE FRAME

Customize your own frame from start to finish to suit the photograph or picture to be mounted. Frame a wedding photograph in rich silk ribbon and colours that enhance the bridal theme. Hold a special Christmas memory within festive red or green and surround a graduation shot in ceremonial brocades. Don't be alarmed if you are not a woodworker. This project requires only basic sawing and stapling. Remember to paint the undercoat in a colour that tones with the ribbons. The finished frame has an approximate picture area of 28 x 20cm (11 x 8in).

1 Mark a point in each corner of the MDF, 4.8cm (1⅞in) from the edges. Drill a small hole at each mark, then cut out the frame between the points using a metal ruler and craft knife.

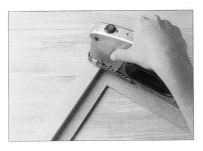

2 Saw the wood strip into four pieces, two of 33cm (13in) and two of 20cm (8in). Sand the ends and glue them in position around the outside edge of the frame. Insert a staple at each joint.

3 Then turn the frame over to the right side and insert ten evenly spaced staples around the frame. Hammer the staples flush with the frame board if necessary. Sand down any rough edges and apply two coats of white undercoat. Allow the paint to dry thoroughly.

4 Cut the ribbon into six 38cm (15in) lengths and six 30cm (12in) lengths. Spread wood glue over the front of the frame. Lay the ribbons on the frame and carefully weave the corners. You may wish to practise this first, before applying the glue.

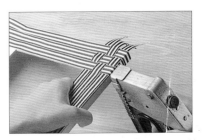

5 Lift the frame on to its side. Fold the ribbon ends over the edge and staple down. Once one end of each ribbon is stapled, pull the other end tightly before stapling. Trim the ribbon ends.

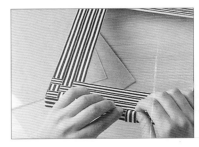

6 Glue the remaining ribbon around the edge of the frame with the join at the base. Staple a small piece of ribbon over the join to conceal it.

Materials and Equipment You Will Need

Piece of MDF (medium-density fiberboard), 33 x 25cm x 2mm (13 x 10 x ⅛in) • Pencil • Metal ruler • Drill • Craft (utility) knife • Wood strip, 106 x 2.5 x 1.25cm (42 x ½ x 1in) • Saw • Sandpaper • Wood glue • Glue spreader or paintbrush • Staple gun and staples • Hammer • White undercoat • Paintbrush • Navy and white striped ribbon, 5.5m x 15mm (6yd x ⅝in)

BATHROOM SET

Pamper yourself and your visitors with these luxurious bathroom accessories that cost little and require minimum effort. Co-ordinating accessories are easily affordable when you brighten up neutral basics with pretty, matching ribbons. The ribbons available today are made to suit any decor: floral, abstract, bright, soft, loud or subtle. Extend the ribbon theme to shower curtains, window drapes and potpourri holders, but remember to check laundry requirements for both the ribbon and the accessory, making sure that they are compatible.

WHITE HAND TOWEL

1 Place pins 2.5cm (1in) apart along the two ends of the towel. Thread a crewel needle with 3mm (⅛in) red ribbon. Insert the needle at one pin and bring out at the next. Knot the ends of the ribbon together neatly so that the ribbon lies flat against the towel. Cut off excess ribbon, leaving tails. Repeat along the edges of the towel.

BLACK MESH BOX

1 Decorate the rim of the lid and base of the box with red ribbon, using the same method as for the towel. Glue starfish or another decorative device around the sides of the box.

2 To make a tassel, bunch together 26 x 38cm (15in) lengths of 3mm (⅛in) red spotted ribbon. Cut two 30cm (12in) lengths of ribbon. Fold one length in half and wrap it around the middle of the bunched ribbons. Thread the ends through the loop and pull tightly.

3 Thread a crewel needle with the other 30cm (12in) length of ribbon. Bind the ribbon tightly around the tassel, then slip the needle behind the binding ribbon and pull tightly. Cut the tassel ends level. Sew the tassel to the centre of the box lid.

WASH MITT

1 If your wash mitt has a strap, cut a length of 9mm (⅜in) black spotted ribbon to fit the strap, adding a small seam allowance at each end. Turn under the seam allowance and stitch the ribbon along the length of the strap. Cut three long lengths of 25mm (1in) black spotted ribbon. Place them on top of each other and tie in a bow around the strap, using the hand-tied method (see Basic Techniques). Pull open each loop of the bow. Decorate soaps, sponges, toothbrushes and cocktail sticks (toothpicks) in the same way, to make a matching set.

Materials and Equipment You Will Need

White hand towel: Dressmaker's pins • Red double-face satin ribbon, 3.5m x 3mm (4yd x ⅛in) • Crewel Needle • Scissors

Black mesh box: Dressmaker's pins • Red spotted double-face satin ribbon, 11.75 m x 3mm (13yd x ⅛in) • Tape measure • Red double-face satin ribbon, 1.5m x 3mm (1⅔yd x ⅛in) • Crewel needle • Scissors • Small red starfish • All-purpose glue • Needle and matching threads

Wash mitt: Black spotted double-face satin ribbon, 25cm x 9mm (10 x ⅜in) • Scissors • Needle and matching thread • Black spotted ribbon, 1.5 m x 25mm (1⅔yd x 1in)

STEMMED TARTAN ROSES

What wouldn't a gardener give to produce roses of such wondrous colours and lasting beauty? Fun to make and bound to be a talking point in any room, these tartan roses can be adapted to suit many occasions. Make them the centrepiece of a festive table or to decorate place settings. Alternatively you can include them in a festive wreath or garland. Stitch a single tartan rose to a plain evening dress or evening bag. These roses are made in the same way as the stitched roses described in the basic techniques section but a stub wire is attached at the beginning.

1 Bend the end of a piece of stub wire to form a hook equal in depth to the ribbon width. Holding the tartan ribbon with the cut end to the right, hook the wire through the upper righthand corner of the ribbon, about 5mm (³⁄₁₆in) from the edge. Close the hook to hold the ribbon.

2 Roll the ribbon around the hook two or three times from right to left to enclose the wire. Stitch to secure (see diagram 1). Then holding the wire stem in your right hand and the loose ribbon in your left, fold the ribbon so that it runs down parallel to the wire (see diagram 2).

3 Roll the covered hook end from right to left into the fold, turning tightly at the bottom and loosely at the top until the ribbon is once again horizontal to the wire.

Diagram 1

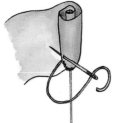

Diagram 2

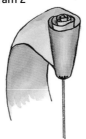

4 With the wire stem facing towards you, stitch the base of the rose to secure it in place. ▶

Materials and Equipment You Will Need

For one rose: Tartan ribbon, 60cm x 39mm (24 x 1¹⁄₂in) • Stub (floral) wire, 20cm (8in) • Needle and matching thread • Craft scissors • Tartan wire-edge ribbon, 30cm x 39mm (12 x 1¹⁄₂in) • Fine florist's wire • Florist's tape (stem wrap)

5 Continue folding the ribbon and rolling the rose in this way, stitching the base after each fold until the desired shape and size of rose are achieved. To complete the rose, cut the ribbon squarely, fold it back neatly on to the rose and stitch lightly to hold in place (see diagram 3).

6 To make the triple leaf, cut the wire-edge ribbon into three equal lengths. Cut three equal lengths of fine florist's wire and make a small loop in each about 2.5cm (1in) from one end.

8 Fold the lower corners of the ribbon triangle under and backwards to create a leaf shape. Gather the lower part of the leaf neatly round the long wire stem and stitch to secure in place.

Diagram 3

7 Fold two corners of a piece of wire-edge ribbon down and forwards to form a triangle. Place one of the pieces of wire centrally in the triangle, with the loop on the lower selvage and the short wire end pointing upwards. Stitch the ribbon to secure the wire in place.

9 Make two more leaves in this way. Bind the wire stems of two of the leaves with florist's tape for about 1.25cm (½in). Bind the wire stem of the third leaf for approximately 2.5cm (1in). Join the three leaves together at this point and continue binding around all three wires to create a single stem. Bind the stem of the tartan rose, binding in the triple leaf about 10cm (4in) down from the rose.

GIFT BOXES

The pleasure given by your gifts will be doubled by these luxurious wrappings that are so easy to achieve. Plain-coloured gift boxes provide the perfect background for ribbon embellishment. You don't need to buy the boxes – make a point of saving cartons and packaging. Paint them in bright colours and add the ribbon. When wrapping Christmas gifts, choose seasonal colours, such as green, red and deep blue for the boxes, and gold and silver ribbons.

LARGE PURPLE GIFT BOX

1 Cut four lengths of green ribbon. Wrap each length around one side of the box and tie in a single loop bow at one corner. Slip each new ribbon under the previous bow. Cut the ribbon ends into chevrons.

RED GIFT BOX

1 Cut a 105cm (42in) length of 39mm (1½in) ribbon and fold it into seven concertina pleats each 15cm (6in) long. Cut the ribbon ends into chevrons. Carefully cut a 1.25cm (½in) nick in the centre of each long side of the folded ribbon. Tie a smaller piece of ribbon around the middle to secure the loops.

2 Open out each fold to make a rounded loop. Hold the bow in place on the gift-box lid. Tuck the ends of the ribbon inside the box lid and glue in place. Cut off the excess ribbon.

►

Materials and Equipment You Will Need
Wire-edge shot taffeta ribbons in various widths • Gift boxes • Scissors • Tape measure • All-purpose glue • Needle and matching threads

GREEN GIFT BOX

1 Wrap a length of purple wire-edge shot-taffeta ribbon around the gift box and cut off, leaving a little extra for tying a knot. Fold the ribbon into small pleats widthways at regular intervals. Secure the pleats in place with neat stitches in matching thread.

2 Wrap the ribbon around the box, gluing in place at the points where the ribbon is tied. Tie the ribbon in a knot close to one corner of the box and cut the ribbon ends in chevrons.

SMALL PURPLE GIFT BOX

1 Glue a length of pink ribbon around the edge of the box lid. Cut two equal lengths of pink ribbon. Glue one end of each ribbon to the inside of the lid on opposite sides. Cut three 38cm (15in) lengths of ribbon. Twist them together in the middle. The wire edge of the ribbon will maintain the shape of the twist. Place the twist in the centre of the box lid. Tie the two glued ribbons together over the twisted ribbons.

2 Knot all the ribbons together and cut the ends diagonally.

BLACK GIFT BOX

1 Cut two lengths of pink ribbon. Tie one length around the box in one direction and the other ribbon in the opposite direction. Holding the ribbons together in pairs, fasten in a single-loop bow. Pull the loops and tails apart. Cut the extending ribbon ends in chevrons.

DRIED FLOWER AND RIBBON WREATH

This traditional floral wreath is easy to make and looks pretty as part of the floral arrangements for a celebration, such as a wedding. The use of dried flowers means that the wreath can be kept for years as a reminder of a happy occasion. For those who prefer a more rigid flower arrangement, apply a little glue to the base of the flower head before pushing the stem into the plastic foam wreath. A glue gun is an excellent tool for this job.

1 Select the dried flowers to blend in well with the gold ribbon.

2 Cut 3cm (1¼in) lengths of stub wire and bend them into 'U' shapes. Cut a piece of ribbon equal in length to twice the circumference of the wreath. Attach one end of the ribbon to the outside of the plastic foam wreath with a stub wire.

3 Stretch the ribbon across its width at regular intervals to create a wavy pattern. Zigzag the ribbon around the top of the ring, securing it at intervals with the pins until you have completed the circle.

4 Stretch the ribbon across its width at regular intervals to create a wavy pattern. Zigzag the ribbon around the top of the ring, securing it at intervals with the pins until you have completed the circle.

5 Insert a second ring of flowers above the first to create a chequered pattern of roses and nigella. Keep checking that you have an even balance all around the wreath. Continue forming circles of flower heads among the gold ribbon until the wreath is covered.

Materials and Equipment You Will Need
Gold mesh wire-edge ribbon, 2m x 39mm (2¼yd x 1½in) • 100 stems dried cream roses • Two bunches dried Nigella orientalis •
Stub (floral) wire, 0.71mm (22g) • Craft scissors • Plastic foam wreath, 21cm (8¼in) in diameter

GOLDEN BRAID CUSHION

Bring an instant lift to a tired furnishing scheme with a touch of dazzling Asian opulence. The rich gold braids are the perfect partner for dark wood furniture or a sombre sofa. Brighten thick velvet curtains with gold tassels to match. The gold braids and ribbons add a luxurious feel, and many interesting colour and textural combinations can be achieved.

1 Ensure that the ticking stripes run parallel to the short sides of the rectangle. Fold in half to find the centre. Cut the braids and ribbons into 40cm (16in) lengths. Starting in the centre and using the woven lines as a guide, sew down lengths of gold braid using a narrow zigzag stitch. Arrange the colours for a dramatic effect and intersperse with red and green satin ribbons to provide contrast. Stitch slowly and carefully to avoid puckering the braid and ribbon.

2 When the ticking is completely covered, press from the back with a cool iron. Trim the edges so that the piece measures 63.5 x 33cm (25 x 13in). Turn under a 1.25cm (½in) allowance on one short edge and hem.

3 Turn under a 1.25cm (½in) allowance on one short edge of the backing fabric and hem. With right sides facing, pin then sew the cushion back and front together along the three raw edges. Clip the corners and turn through.

4 Press the fabric lightly and insert the cushion pad. Slip stitch the fourth edge closed (see Basic Techniques).

5 Slip stitch the furnishing cord around the edge of the cushion, making a small decorative loop at each corner.

Materials and Equipment You Will Need

Striped ticking 75 x 40cm (30 x 16in) • About 18 different patterned gold braids, 1m (40in) of each • Red and green satin ribbons, 1.75m x 15mm (2yd x ⅝in) • Tape measure • Scissors • Needle and matching threads • Iron • Co-ordinating backing fabric, 63.5 x 33cm (25 x 13in) • Cushion pad, 60 x 30cm (24 x 12in) • Heavy gold furnishing cord, 1.75m (2yd)

BALLET SHOES

Aspiring prima ballerinas will be delighted with the effect that silky satin ribbon has on plain ballet pumps. Ballet slippers are also often worn at balls or among bridal parties; and what simpler way to create that co-ordinated look from top to toe than matching ribbon roses on gowns, shoes and accessories? Allow about 10cm (4in) of ribbon per rose for the shoes. Refer to the basic techniques for ribbon requirements for larger roses.

1 Roll the raw end of a length of 9mm (⅜in) ribbon inward to the left two or three times. Stitch neatly at the lower edge to secure.

2 Holding the stitched end in your right hand and the loose ribbon in your left, fold the ribbon away from you so that

the tail hangs down (see Stemmed Tartan Roses). Roll the stitched end from right to left, turning tightly at the bottom and more loosely at the top to form a petal. The ribbon should be horizontal. Stitch to secure the petal.

3 Continue folding the ribbon, rolling the rose and stitching each petal until the rose is of the desired size. Cut the ribbon square about 5mm (³⁄₁₆in) from the rose. Fold the end neatly on to the rose and stitch to secure. Make five more roses in toning shades.

4 Stitch a cluster of three roses, one rose of each shade, to the front of each shoe.

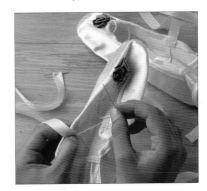

5 Cut the 15mm (⅝in) ribbon into four equal lengths. Stitch one length inside each side of the ballet shoes to form ties. Neatly hem the end of each tie to prevent fraying.

Materials and Equipment You Will Need
Three toning shades of doubleface satin ribbon, 20cm x 9mm (8 x ⅜in) of each • Needle and matching threads • Scissors • Pair of ballet shoes • Single-face satin ribbon to match ballet shoes, about 2m x 15mm (2¼yd x ⅝in)

RIBBON JEWELLERY

Ribbon has many advantages, not least its versatility. Here pieces of richly patterned ribbon are fashioned into a stunning necklace. Make a double strand or, using shorter pieces, make a matching bracelet. Other accessories and jewellery pieces can be made using the same technique. Attach ribbon tubes to a brooch back or hairslide (barrette), adorn a plain bag with one or two, or stitch a group to the brim of a hat and embellish with frothy sheer ribbon.

1 Cut six 7 x 4cm (2¾ x 1½in) rectangles from the card and roll into tubes.

2 Cut six 6.5cm (2½in) strips of patterned ribbon, selecting the pattern area you want to use along the ribbon. Glue one end of each piece of ribbon on to the outside end of each tube of paper.

3 Fold over the other end of the ribbon by 5mm (¼in). Roll the ribbon around the tube so that the edges of the ribbon meet. Stitch down the join. Push the wired edges of the ribbon into the tube.

4 Apply glue to both ends of the covered tubes and press a bead on to each end. Hold the beads in place while the glue dries by threading a piece of wire through each tube and bending the end around.

5 Thread the ribbon-covered tubes on to the 3mm (⅛in) ribbon with gold and coloured beads in between.

6 Thread a clasp on to the ends of the ribbon. Fold each ribbon end back on itself and stitch down, wrapping the thread over the stitching. Knot the end of the ribbon and wrap again with thread to cover the knot. Secure the thread firmly before cutting it off.

Materials and Equipment You Will Need
Thin white card (stock) • Pencil • Ruler • Scissors • Wire-edge patterned ribbon, 39cm x 50mm (15½ x 2in) • Epoxy resin glue • Glue spreader or paintbrush • Needle and matching thread • Round and tubular beads, 1.5cm (⅝in) wide • Plastic-coated garden wire • Toning ribbon, about 75cm x 3mm (30 x ⅛in) • Small gold beads • Necklace clasp

RIBBON LANTERN

Unusual lanterns add colour and character to a room. Lantern frames are available in many different shapes and sizes so you can adapt the basic idea. To show the lantern to its full effect, the ribbons should butt up closely around each side. Measure around all four sides of the frame and then select a width of ribbon which can be multiplied to fit into this measurement exactly. The length of ribbon you use for each strand will also vary according to the delicacy and style of the frame and the finished look

1 Cut lengths of ribbon twice as long as they will appear on the finished lantern. To mitre one end of each ribbon, turn in lcm (⅜in) along the raw edge and press lightly with a dry iron to hold in place.

2 Fold in one corner to the centre of the ribbon, then fold in the other corner. Iron to hold in position.

3 Thread a needle and tie a knot in one end. Pass the needle through the point of the mitre, then thread a small bead followed by a larger bead on to the needle. Tie a large knot in the end of the thread to hold the beads in place and, if it is necessary, add a little glue to the base of the large bead.

4 Slip stitch along the central join of the mitre, keeping a neat point at the end of the mitre (see Basic Techniques).

5 Turn the other end of the ribbon over, and loop the ribbon over one side of the frame. Slip stitch the second end of the ribbon to the top of the mitre, making sure that the wrong sides of the ribbon will be on the inside of the frame. Make all the other ribbons in this way.

Materials and Equipment You Will Need
Basic lantern frame • Tape measure • Ribbon, length and width depending on size of frame • Scissors • Iron • Needle and matching threads • Beads (one small and one large per ribbon) • PVA (white) glue

ROLL-UP NEEDLEWORK CASE

This handy roll-up case brings together different aspects of needlework: patchwork, embroidery and sewing. The crazy design will be unique for every case made and requires little planning. Adapt the size of the case and pockets to suit your own purposes. The case would make an ideal travel kit or stationery holder, or use it to hold your craft equipment or art materials. The use of canvas makes the case very sturdy, though if you intend to make a holder for heavier equipment, choose a heavyweight canvas. Adapt the pockets to suit larger tools.

1 Cut the canvas into four rectangles, two measuring 30 x 20cm (12 x 8in) and two 30 x 10cm (12 x 4in).

2 Cut the toning ribbons into various lengths of between 2.5–7.5cm (1–3in).

3 Use running stitch or back stitch to sew the ribbon pieces on to one of the 30 x 20cm (12 x 8in) canvas rectangles, turning under the raw edges (see Basic Techniques). Continue until the entire panel is covered. Don't worry about any small gaps. These add to the crazy patchwork look and can be filled with embroidery stitches.

4 Oversew the edges of the patchwork pieces using three or four different embroidery threads and a range of stitches. Cross stitch, running stitch and chain stitch all work well.

►

Materials and Equipment You Will Need
Lightweight canvas, 50cm (20in) • Pencil • Ruler • Scissors • Five different toning ribbons, 1m (40in) of each • Needle and matching threads • Toning embroidery threads (flosses) • Dressmaker's pins • Ribbon for binding, 1.5m x 25mm (1⅔yd x 1in) • Ribbon for ties, 50cm x 5mm (½yd x ³/₁₆in)

5 Work blanket stitch around three edges of one of the 30 x 10cm (12 x 4in) rectangles, leaving one of the long edges unsewn.

7 Blanket stitch along the top edge of the pocket panel. Position this on the second 30 x 20cm (12 x 8in) piece of canvas and join the two panels together with running stitch or back stitch along the pocket lines.

9 Place the remaining rectangle above the pocket piece to form a flap, with the unsewn edge at the top. Pin in place and bind the top edge with ribbon as described in step eight.

6 Using a pencil and ruler, draw the lines of the pockets on the second 30 x 10cm (12 x 4in) rectangle. Size the pockets according to the embroidery tools you wish to carry.

8 To assemble the embroidery case, place the patchwork panel face down on the work surface. Place the pocket piece on top with the pocket side facing you. Pin or tack (baste) together and bind the bottom and side edges with the 25mm (1in) ribbon. Use a small running stitch or back stitch to secure the ribbon, stitching through all the layers.

10 Fold the length of 5mm (3⁄16in) ribbon in half and at the centre point stitch it inside one side edge of the case. Use this ribbon to secure the needlework case, when rolled up.

CLASSIC EVENING PURSE

This luxurious evening purse exudes style and dainty elegance. The velvet fabric is painted with stripes of gold, insertions are cut into the velvet along the edges of each stripe and then toning ribbons are threaded through the slits. This unique idea is guaranteed to steal the show for accessory style. The technique could easily be adapted to suit larger projects such as a waistcoat or evening shawl. What show stoppers those would be!

1 Enlarge the pattern pieces on page 94 to size. A seam allowance of 1.25cm (½in) is included. Cut two of the larger rectangles from black velvet, two of the smaller rectangles from black lining fabric and one circle from each fabric.

2 Place one rectangle of velvet fabric face up on a large sheet of paper (to protect the work surface). Lay vertical strips of

masking tape over the velvet, leaving 2.5cm (1in) between the strips. Lay a double strip of masking tape horizontally across the centre of the fabric.

3 Apply gold paint lightly and evenly to the exposed areas of fabric. Remove the tape and follow the manufacturer's instructions for fixing the paint.

4 To make a template for the ribbon insertions, cut a strip of thin card to the length of the painted stripes on one half of the velvet. Mark one edge of the card at six regular intervals. Position the template alongside one of the painted stripes and mark the cutting points on the velvet using a dressmaker's felt-tipped pen. Continue to mark cutting points in this way on either side of each stripe. Only mark the bottom half of the whole piece of velvet.

5 Using sharp-pointed scissors, cut 5mm (³⁄₁₆in) slits in the fabric at the marked points.

▶

Materials and Equipment You Will Need

Black velvet, 40 x 40cm (16 x 16in) • Black lining fabric, 20 x 20cm (8 x 8in) • Scissors • Large sheet of paper • Masking tape, 25mm (1in) wide • Gold fabric paint • Paintbrush • Thin card (stock) • Dressmaker's felt-tipped pen • Small sharp-pointed scissors • Silver ribbon, 1.6m x 5mm (1¾yd x ³⁄₁₆in) • Green ribbon, 1.75m x 5mm (2yd x ³⁄₁₆in) • Maroon ribbon, 1.75m x 5mm (2yd x ³⁄₁₆in) • Tape measure • Tapestry needle • Dressmaker's pins • Needle and matching threads • Iron

6 Cut the ribbons into 20cm (8in) lengths: four lengths of silver, two of green and two of maroon. Use a tapestry needle to thread the ribbon through each row of slits, changing the colour with each row. Thread the ribbon loosely, allowing it to fall naturally.

7 Secure the ends of each ribbon on the back of the velvet with a few stitches. Repeat steps two to six with the second rectangle of black velvet.

8 With right sides facing, pin, tack (baste) and sew the two rectangles together down the long sides, leaving a small gap in the middle of each side as shown on the pattern. Sew both lining rectangles together along the short edges, leaving a small opening in the middle of one side unstitched for turning.

9 With right sides facing, pin, tack and sew the long sides of the lining to the upper edge of the bag, matching up the seam lines. Press and stitch the seam.

10 Turn the bag inside out and, with right sides facing, sew the circle of velvet to the bottom edges of the bag. Sew the circle of lining fabric to the bottom edges of the lining.

11 Turn the bag through the openings to the right side. Fold along the fold line and press gently. Tack along the stitching lines indicated on the pattern to form the drawstring channel, then stitch. Close the side opening with slip stitches (see Basic Techniques). Thread green and maroon ribbon through the channel to form a drawstring. Tie a knot in each ribbon to secure.

CELEBRATION CAKE

Commemorate a special occasion with a highly unusual celebration cake. This cone-shaped cake is decorated with ribbon and iced ornaments. Beneath each ornament is a ribbon loop made from icing. Marzipan is easier to roll in small sections between sheets of plastic or clear film (plastic wrap). Piece the sections together on the cake. When handling the marzipan, wrap clear film around your hands to prevent the marzipan from sticking to the rolling pin or your fingers.

1 Place the largest layer of cake on the cake board and stack the other layers on top, sticking them with apricot jam (jelly). Trim down the sides with a large serrated knife to form a cone shape. Roll a piece of marzipan to make the tip of the cone. Brush the cake all over with apricot jam and cover with a layer of marzipan about 5mm (³⁄₁₆in) thick. Leave the cake to dry overnight.

2 Prepare the royal icing with icing sugar, egg white and lemon juice. Set some aside in a small bowl for the decorations. Add a few drops of glycerine to the remainder. Ice the cake with a layer of icing, smoothing it with a metal spatula. Set the cake aside. Using a small paper piping bag or a very

fine nozzle, and the glycerine-free icing, pipe 20 to 30 rectangular loops on to sheets of baking parchment. Leave to set overnight.

3 Using the templates on page 93 as a guide, ice the ornaments on to sheets of baking parchment. Decorate one or two with dragée almonds or chocolates and leave to set overnight.

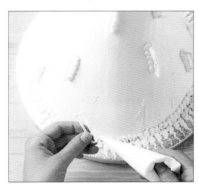

4 The next day, ice the cake with a second layer of icing. Two coats of icing should be sufficient, but a third is sometimes required for extra whiteness. Add decorative piping around the bottom edge of the cake. When you are satisfied with the finish of the icing, start to position the

loops on the freshly iced cake. Pipe a little icing on to one long side of each loop to fix it to the cake. Starting at the bottom, fix four or five spiralling circles of loops to the cake, spacing them evenly. Leave overnight.

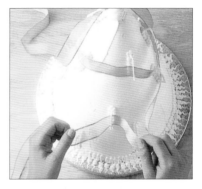

5 Thread the gold ribbon through all the loops. Add a decoration to each loop by piping on a little icing to fix it. If you prefer, any visible cake board can be covered with extra ribbon or a combination of fresh flowers, ivy and ribbon.

Materials and Equipment You Will Need
For about 60 people: Four layers of matured, rich fruitcake, 7.5, 13, 18 and 23cm (3, 5, 7 and 9in) in diameter and 7cm (3in) high • Cake board • Apricot jam (jelly) • Serrated knife • Rolling pin • Pastry brush • Marzipan • Plastic sheets or clear film (plastic wrap) • Royal icing with glycerine • Royal icing without glycerine • Metal spatula • Piping bags • Icing nozzles • Baking parchment • Dragée almonds or chocolates • Wire-edge sheer gold ribbon, 1.75m x 25–39mm (2yd x 1–1¹⁄₂in) • Fresh flowers (optional) • Ivy (optional)

POTPOURRI BAG

This perennial project takes on a new guise with simple ribbon embroidery that even the newest craftworker can manage to pleasing effect. To vary the bag, embroider multicoloured flowers directly on to striped cotton and tie with matching ribbon. Enlarge the pot-pourri bag to make a lavender or herb cushion, an unusual gift that is sure to please. Add a half lining to the sachet to give extra thickness around the tied neck area. The lining can be extended to line the entire bag – simply use the waffle- fabric measurement, adding extra for seam allowances.

1 Place the fabric in an embroidery hoop. Starting 10cm (4in) in from one long edge, work a row of eight lazy daisy stitch flowers in deep blue, pink, purple and yellow ribbon (see Basic Techniques) over 20cm (8in). Space them evenly and make each flower 2cm (¾in) in diameter. Work a small French knot in the centre of each flower. Press the fabric lightly and trim to 25 x 20cm (10 x 8in) so that the flowers lie 7.5cm (3in) from the bottom edge.

2 Thread the needle with emerald green ribbon and weave two horizontal lines through the top threads of the fabric to form a border on either side of the flowers. With bright blue ribbon, weave seven vertical lines to form a striped pattern. There is no need to knot the ribbon at each end.

3 With right sides facing, pin then stitch the green and white fabric along the top

edge of the waffle fabric, leaving a 1.25cm (½in) seam allowance. Open out and press the seam.

4 Fold the whole piece in half vertically with the right sides of the embroidery facing and the right sides of the lining facing. Pin and stitch the side seam along the long edge. Pin and stitch along the bottom edge. Clip the corners and turn to the right side. Push the green lining to the inside and press the top edge.

5 Fill the bag with potpourri. Complete by tying the remaining ribbons into a bow around the neck of the bag.

Materials and Equipment You Will Need
White loose-weave waffle fabric, 30 x 25cm (12 x 10in) • Embroidery hoop • Deep blue, pink, purple and yellow satin ribbons, 1m x 3mm (1yd x ⅛in) of each • Chenille needle • Scissors • Iron • Emerald green satin ribbon, 70cm x 3mm (27½ x ⅛in) • Bright blue satin ribbon, 1.75m x 3mm (2yd x ⅛in) • Green and white striped fabric, 25 x 12.75cm (10 x 5in) • Dressmaker's pins • Matching thread • Potpourri

BASKET-WEAVE CUSHION

The open-weave technique worked on this cushion cover allows the beauty of the dark blue moiré taffeta backing fabric to show through the complementing richness of the woven brocade, velvet and jacquard ribbons. Weaving can be used in a great many ways to make clothing, such as the Woven Ribbon Waistcoat project and an endless variety of furnishing accessories. Other weaving techniques and designs are described in the Basic Techniques section. Experiment with the different designs to make a set of co-ordinating cushions in the same or toning colours.

1 Cut a 35.5cm (14in) square of blue taffeta. Fold in four to find the centre and open out. Cut all the ribbons into 35.5cm (14in) lengths. Start the weaving by placing one length of black rosebud brocade vertically down the centre of the taffeta. Place a length of claret rosebud brocade horizontally across the black ribbon. Pin these ribbons to the taffeta at the point where they cross and at each end. Place a claret velvet ribbon either side of each ribbon, leaving 5mm (³⁄₁₆in) between the ribbons. Lay the vertical ribbon over the claret rosebud brocade and weave the horizontal ribbons over the vertical velvet ribbons and under the black rosebud brocade. Pin the points where the ribbons cross to hold them (see Basic Techniques).

2 Using a ruler to ensure that all the lines are straight, continue to weave in the other ribbons, following the design of the finished cushion. When the weave is complete, pin all the loose ribbon ends to the taffeta backing fabric.

3 Starting at one edge, sew the ribbons to the taffeta by making two small, neat

overstitches across each point where the ribbons overlap. Sew the ribbons firmly in place but avoid pulling the thread too tightly across the back, as this will distort the weave.

4 Cut two rectangles of taffeta 35.5 x 25cm (14 x 10in). Fold under a 1.25cm (½in) allowance along one long side of each rectangle. Press and fold the same allowance again and stitch a hem. Place the two rectangles on the woven piece with right sides facing, to form a cushion back. Overlap the two hemmed edges. Stitch around all four edges, using a 1.25cm (1in) seam allowance. Clip the corners and turn through to the right side. Press lightly, using a pressing cloth to protect the velvet ribbon, and insert the cushion pad.

Materials and Equipment You Will Need
Dark blue moiré taffeta, 1m x 38cm (40 x 15in) • Scissors • Ruler • Black rosebud brocade, 1.15m x 19mm (1¼yd x ¾in) • Claret rosebud brocade, 1.15m x 19mm (1¼yd x ¾in) • Dressmaker's pins • Claret velvet ribbon, 1.15m x 23mm (1¼yd x ⅞in) • Purple marble-print ribbon, 1.15m x 23mm (1¼yd x ⅞in) • Dark red ribbon, 1.15m x 25mm (1¼yd x 1in) • Claret jacquard ribbon, 1.15m x 7mm (1¼yd x ¼in) • Green velvet ribbon, 2.5m x 19mm (2¾yd x ¾in) • Needle and matching threads • Iron and pressing cloth • Cushion pad, 30 x 30cm (12 x 12in)

CLOCHE HAT

Ribbons can be used in numerous ways to brighten up both summer and winter hats. Here, ribbon plays a functional and ornamental role in this fun accessory as it reinforces the structure of the hat and forms the decorative band. The flowers are made from circles of fabric stuffed with wadding surrounded by gathered ribbon petals.

1 Cut out several leaves from the green felt. Machine stitch around the leaves with green thread and add veins.

2 Reinforce the wide black ribbon with a strip of iron-on interfacing. Arrange some leaves on the ribbon and machine stitch in place.

3 Make flowers by cutting out circles from the scraps of fabric and cotton wool or wadding, using the templates on page 93 as a guide. Place a piece of wadding on each piece of fabric and work a running stitch around the edge of the fabric circle (see Basic Techniques). Gather the thread tightly to form the flower centre and stitch to secure. Sew on a few beads. Gather 23cm (9in) of pink ribbon around each flower centre and stitch in place. For the smaller flowers, fold 14cm (5½in) of ribbon in half lengthways. Work a running stitch along the fold and gather tightly.

4 Pin the flowers on to the ribbon between the leaves and stitch in place.

5 Drape some net over the hat. Pin it to the brim and stitch in place.

6 Attach the decorated band of ribbon to the brim. Decorate the crown with small flowers and leaves.

Materials and Equipment You Will Need

Cloche hat • Small pieces of light and dark green felt • Scissors • Sewing machine • Green thread • Black velvet ribbon, 50mm (2in) wide and long enough to go around the hat • Strip of iron-on interfacing • Iron • Scraps of fine fabric • Cotton wool or wadding (batting) • Needle and matching threads • Beads • Pink ribbon, 2m x 25mm (2¼yd x 1in) • Dressmaker's pins • Millinery net, 50cm (40in)

CHRISTMAS DECORATIONS

These subtle Christmas decorations make a welcome change from glitzy store-bought baubles and tinsel. The earthy colours complement the natural beauty of a Christmas tree or holly wreath, while the use of gold ribbon gives the decorations a luxurious seasonal glow. Small presents or boxes can be wrapped in the same way as the pine- cone parcels. Hang the decorations on the tree or along a length of gold ribbon to string across a mantelpiece.

BAUBLES

1 Use a pencil to divide a polystyrene ball into quarters vertically, then into eights with a horizontal line around the middle. Place a length of ribbon across one section, pin at each end on the drawn lines and cut off the ribbon. Continue filling in the section, using the assorted ribbons like patchwork, overlapping the ribbon edges and laying the ribbon smoothly over the ball.

2 Fill in all the sections, completely covering the ball. Lay the patterned ribbon along the lines that were drawn as a guide, covering the pins and ribbon ends. Pin in position at each point where the pencil lines cross, turning the ribbon ends under to neaten. To make a loop for hanging the bauble, slip a 25cm (10in) length of ribbon under one intersection. Knot the ends together.

3 Take several gold lace pins and slip a tiny gold bead followed by a gold-coin pendant on to each one. Pin them in a row around the bauble. Thread a small bead and then a large, ornate bead on to the last pin and stick it into the base of the bauble to complete. Make other baubles in the same way but using different coloured threads.

►

Materials and Equipment You Will Need
Baubles: Polystyrene (Styrofoam) balls, 7.5 or 5cm (3 or 2in) in diameter • Pencil • Tape measure • Gold, brown and cream ribbons, 1m x 3–9mm (40 in x ⅛–⅜in) oDressmaker's pins • Scissors • Toning patterned ribbon, 2m x 3–9mm (2¼yd x ⅛–⅜in) • Gold lace pins • Gold-coin pendants • Tiny gold beads • Large, ornate gold beads
Pine cone parcels: Gold, lemon or brown ribbon, 39mm (1½in) wide • Gold or brown ribbon, 3mm (⅛in) wide • Pine cones • PVA (white) glue
Golden tassel: Cotton-pulp ball, 2.5cm (1in) in diameter • Scissors • Gold grosgrain ribbon, 9.9m x 3mm (11yd x ⅛in) • Crewel needle • PVA (white) glue

PINE-CONE PARCELS

1 Make a hand-tied bow with the wide ribbon (see Basic Techniques). Wrap the narrow ribbon around the pine cone as if wrapping a parcel. Tie the ribbon at the top of the cone. Dab with glue to secure. Tie the ribbon ends together 10cm (4in) above the top of the cone to make a hanging loop. Glue the bow on top of the cone to complete.

GOLDEN TASSEL

1 Use scissors to make a hole through the centre of the cotton-pulp ball. Pull out some of the fibre to enlarge the hole to 1.25cm (½in) in diameter.

2 Cut a 25cm (10in) length from the ribbon and cut the remainder into 30cm (12in) lengths. Put the 25cm (10in) length and one 30cm (12in) length to one side and insert the remainder through the hole, a few at a time. Use the crewel needle to thread them through if necessary. Allow 12.5cm (5in) of each ribbon to hang below the ball. Dab a little glue on to the ball and fold down the ribbons protruding from the top around the outside of the ball. Continue until the ball is completely covered.

3 Thread the needle with the 25cm (10in) length of ribbon. Glue one end around the ribbons close to the base of the ball. Wrap the ribbon tightly around the tassel.

4 Insert the needle behind the binding ribbon and pull tightly. Unthread the needle, allowing the ribbon end to hang down with the other ribbons. Do not trim at this stage.

5 To suspend the tassel, double the 30cm (12in) length of ribbon and thread it on to the needle. Insert the needle down through the hole in the ball. Remove the needle, knot the ends neatly together and trim the ends. Gently pull the loop taut, hiding the knot among the ribbons. Trim the ribbon ends to an even length.

FRESH FLOWER AND RIBBON HEADDRESS

Fresh flowers require more attention than dried and it is important to 'condition' the flowers before making the headdress. Trim the stems and give the flowers a long drink before use. The florist's tape holds in water as well as concealing any wires. The headdress can be made the day before it is required if it is kept in a cool refrigerator; the flowers should not touch the sides of the refrigerator. The finished headdress can be misted lightly but take care to avoid wetting the ribbon.

1 Cut the stems of the Aronia berry clusters to about 5mm (3/16in). To double leg mount the clusters, cut short lengths of 0.38mm (28g) stub wire. Hold the stem of the cluster between your thumb and index finger. Position a length of stub wire behind and at a right angle to the stem, one third of the way up. Bend the wire down into a 'U' shape so that one leg is twice as long as the other.

2 Holding the shorter leg against the stem, wrap the longer leg around both the stem and the other wire a couple of times.

Straighten both legs, which should now be about the same length and in line with the stem. Double leg mount the clusters of Hydrangea florets, the Leycesteria flowers and the small roses in the same way.

3 Wire each Lizianthus flower head by piercing the seedbox with a length of stub wire. Push it about one third of the way through, then bend the wire legs down and wrap the legs around the stem as described for double leg mounting.

4 Remove the flower heads of the Antirrhinum from the main stem. Cut two short lengths of stub wire for each of the heads. Bend one of the wires in half and twist at the bend to create a small loop above the two legs. Push the two legs down the throat of the flower and out at the base to create a stem. The loop sits in the narrowest part of the flower, preventing the wire from pulling all the way through.

5 Use the second piece of wire to double leg mount the protruding wire and any natural stem.

▶

Materials and Equipment You Will Need
12 Small clusters of Aronia melanocarpa berries • Scissors • Stub (floral) wire, 0.38mm (28g) • 12 Small clusters of Hydrangea florets • 12 Leycesteria formosa flower heads • Small garden roses • 12 Lizianthus flower heads • 12 Single Antirrhinum florets • Florist's tape (stem wrap) • Burgundy sheer ribbon, 8m x 23mm (8³/₄yd x ⁷/₈in) • Tape measure • Stub (floral) wire, 0.71mm (22g)

6 Cover the stems and wires of all the flowers using florist's tape. Between the thumb and index finger of your left hand, hold the end of a length of tape against the top of the flower stem. With your left hand, hold the rest of the tape at a right angle to the stem, keeping it taut. Start wrapping from the top, rotating the stem slowly as you work your way down. By keeping the tape taut, it will stretch into a thin layer around the stem and wires. Overlap the florist's tape as you work, pressing it firmly to secure in place.

7 Make 14 three-loop ribbon bows, each with two tails. For each bow cut a 55cm (21½in) length of ribbon and divide it into six equal sections. Fold the ribbon concertina-style, pinching the folds together at the base. Double leg mount each bow using stub wire.

8 To make a stay wire on which to build the headdress, cut several equal lengths of the thicker stub wire. Group four wires together so that each overlaps the next by about 3cm (1¼in). Starting at one end, use florist's tape to bind the wires securely together.

9 As the tape reaches the end of the first wire, add another piece of wire to the remaining three and continue binding. Continue adding more wires and binding until the stay wire measures about 4cm (1½in) more than the circumference of the wearer's head.

10 Starting at one end, tape the wired flowers securely to the stay wire in your chosen arrangement.

11 Continue taping the flowers along the stay wire, curving the wire as you work. Finish about 4cm (1½in) from the end.

12 Overlap the undecorated end of the stay wire with the decorated beginning. Tape the wires together under the flowers.

CHRISTENING PILLOW

Create an heirloom gift combining the freshness of pure white cotton with the silky soft appeal of ribbon embroidery in delicate pastels. Duplicate the embroidery design on a cot quilt for a pretty but practical duo that will see service for many years. This type of ribbon embroidery is easy to work and can produce wonderfully lifelike effects, but refer to the tips in the Basic Techniques section if you have never tried it before.

1 Cut a 23 x 23cm (9 x 9in) square of cotton piqué and iron the interfacing to one side. Transfer the garland design on page 93 to the fabric by tracing it through dressmaker's carbon paper or by drawing freehand with a vanishing fabric pen. Mount the fabric in an embroidery hoop. Work the roses first by stitching a star shape of four overlapping straight stitches in pale pink. With darker pink ribbon, work a circle of overlapping, slightly longer stitches around the centre to give the effect of petals. Work a few more stitches at one side to give depth to the rose.

2 Using the various shades of green ribbon, work the leaves in straight stitch and the rosebuds in lazy daisy stitch. Work a single pink straight stitch for the centre of each rosebud and fill any spaces with small French knots. Work the rest of the garland design using a range of formal and random stitches. The complete pillow will act as a guide but need not be followed too rigidly. Trim the finished piece to a 15 x 15cm (6 x 6in) square. Finish with a small, single loop bow made from a piece of 5mm (³⁄₁₆in) ribbon.

3 Cut four 9 x 9cm (3½ x 3½in) squares of cotton piqué. Cut four 15 x 9cm (6 x 3½in) rectangles. Cut the broderie anglaise insertion into four 9cm (3½in), two 15cm (6in) and two 33cm (13in) lengths. Edge one side of each square and one long side of two of the rectangles using a 1.25cm (½in) seam allowance. Sew the insertion-edged rectangles to opposite sides of the embroidered square. Sew an insertion-edged square to either end of the two remaining rectangles (see diagram 1, page 86).

▶

Materials and Equipment You Will Need

White cotton piqué, 90 x 30cm (36 x 12in) • Scissors • Tape measure • Lightweight iron-on interfacing, 23 x 23cm (9 x 9in) • Iron • Dressmaker's carbon paper or vanishing fabric pen • Embroidery hoop • Chenille needle • Satin ribbon in pale pink, mid-pink, dusky pink, pale mint-green, pale lime-green, pale aqua, 1.75m x 3mm (2yd x ⅛in) of each • Ribbon, 1.4m x 5mm (1½yd x ³⁄₁₆in) • Narrow broderie anglaise insertion, 1.4m (1½yd) • Broderie anglaise edging, 1.4m x 75mm (1½yd x 3in) • Dressmaker's pins • Needle and matching and contrasting threads • Tapestry needle • Cushion pad, 30 x 30cm (12 x 12in)

Diagram 1

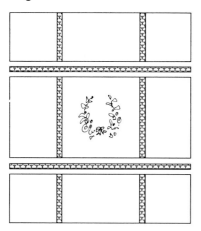

4 Use the two remaining strips of broderie anglaise insertion to join all three strips together, thus framing the embroidered square. Press the seam allowance towards the central square on the wrong side.

5 Join the two ends of the broderie anglaise edging and run a gathering thread along the raw edge. Fold the edging into four equal sections, marking each quarter division with a small scissor cut. Pin each of these cuts to one corner of the pillow top on the right side. Draw up the gathering thread to fit the cushion. Distribute the gathers evenly, allowing a little more fullness at the corners. Pin the broderie anglaise around the outside edge so that it lies on top of the cushion. Tack (baste) and sew in place.

6 Thread the 5mm (³⁄₁₆in) ribbon through the insertion using the tapestry needle, securing each end with a few tacking (basting) stitches.

7 Cut a 30 x 30cm (12 x 12in) square of cotton piqué for the pillow back. Pin to the right side of the pillow front, ensuring that the lace is free of the seam line. Sew around three sides then turn to the right side. Insert the cushion pad and slip stitch the fourth side closed.

WOVEN RIBBON WAISTCOAT

Dressmaking skills are required for this project and a sewing machine is desirable, although not essential. The lined waistcoat shown is a medium, adult size. Ribbon requirements will have to be adjusted up or down for other sizes. Ensure the waistcoat pattern selected does not require darts in the front panels. You could add woven pockets to the waistcoat, with the weaving running in a different direction or using a narrower ribbon.

1 Lay the iron-on interfacing, glue side down, on top of the waistcoat front pattern piece. Cut the interfacing around the pattern. Transfer the markings to the interfacing. Turn the pattern piece over and repeat to cut out the second waistcoat front. Draw two crossing diagonal lines as a guide for weaving.

2 Lay the interfacing on a board, glue side up, and secure with masking tape. Using the pencil lines as a guide, lay and cut

ribbons side by side in one diagonal direction overlapping the edges. Tape or pin one long ribbon on the opposite diagonal at both ends and weave lengths of ribbon (see Basic Techniques).

3 Weave in lengths of ribbon to cover the whole piece of interfacing. You will have to keep adjusting the ribbons to make sure the pattern is neat. Cut the ribbons so that they overlap the edges of the interfacing.

4 Continue weaving until the interfacing is covered. Press with a dry iron. Remove the tape, turn over and press again with a steam iron or under a damp cloth.

5 Trim the ribbons to the edge of the interfacing. Iron an extra strip of interfacing to the front edge of each piece to provide a firm base for the buttonholes and buttons. Overlap the seamline slightly.

Materials and Equipment You Will Need
Commercial waistcoat pattern • Iron-on interfacing • Scissors • Pencil or dressmaker's pencil • Ruler • Masking tape •
Gold ribbon, about 20m x 25mm (22¼yd x 1in) • Dressmaker's pins • Steam iron or dry iron and damp cloth • Small gold beads •
Needle and matching threads • Blue lining fabric, 1.5m x 115cm (1⅔yd x 45in) • Sewing machine • Three buttons

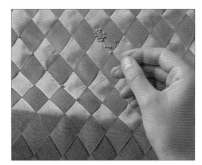

6 Using a double thread with a knot at the end, sew a small gold bead to each point where the ribbons cross. Work along the diagonal and keep the seam allowances free of beads. Secure each bead with a double stitch before going on to the next bead.

8 Cut two 60cm (24in) lengths of ribbon for the back ties. Fold in half to make two 30cm (12in) lengths and sew down both sides, stitching in the same direction to avoid puckering. Pin the raw ends of the ties in place on the waistcoat back and stitch. Trim the raw ends to 5mm (³⁄₁₆in) and fold back. Secure firmly in place.

10 Trim and press the seam open. Fold the lining seam allowance inside and slip stitch closed (see Basic Techniques). Sew the side seams in the same way. Slip stitch the bottom edge of the waistcoat back closed.

7 Cut two back pieces (one outer back and one back lining) and one of each front piece from the blue lining fabric. Mark the position of the back ties and buttonholes. Pin and sew the front lining and woven front pieces together, right sides facing. Stitch around the front edge, along the bottom and around the armhole seams, leaving the shoulder and side seams open. Trim the seams and corners, clipping the curves and turning them in. If machining, use a zipper foot to avoid squashing the beads. Turn the waistcoat to the right side.

9 Join the waistcoat back to the back lining with right sides facing. Stitch along the neck and around the armholes. Trim and clip seam allowances and turn to the right side. With right sides facing, sew the front and back together along the shoulder seams, but only stitch through one layer, leaving the linings free.

11 Make three buttonholes. Use gold-coloured thread on top of the machine and blue in the spool case, so that the thread matches the fabric on both sides. Snip the buttonholes and sew the buttons in position.

RIBBON-EMBROIDERED SAMPLER

This pretty, traditional sampler is worked in the unconventional medium of ribbon, giving the stitches an attractive raised finish. Refer to the tips for ribbon embroidery in the Basic Techniques section before you begin working the sampler. Remember to try to recreate the natural look of flowers, leaves and stems with ribbon embroidery. Concentrate on achieving a realistic look rather than perfect, symmetrical stitches. The basket of roses is fun to work and, as no two roses will ever look exactly alike, the effect is quite natural.

1 Oversew the edges of the Aida cloth in contrasting thread. Find the centre of the cloth by stitching a vertical and horizontal line through the centre.

2 Place the cloth in an embroidery hoop. Following the chart, count from the centre of the cloth to begin working the letter 'W' in pastel green. Work all the letters in cross stitch, ensuring that the stitches are all worked in the same direction for a neat finish. Work French knots with violet ribbon in the spaces left in each letter (see Basic Techniques).

3 Start the basket by sewing long straight stitches in sable ribbon, following the chart. Work stitches over your finger to help keep them flat. Bring the needle up at the same side of the basket for each stitch to maintain the tension.

4 Work a long loose stitch for the handle and arrange it in a loop. Anchor the

handle at two points with a rosebud and leaves. Then bring the needle up at the top of the basket and weave through the straight stitches from top to bottom. Take the needle through to the back at the bottom and back up at the top ready for the next weaving stitch.

5 Then sew the roses inside the basket (see Basic Techniques). Finish off the basket, then sew the numbers below in cross stitch.

▶

Materials and Equipment You Will Need

14-count cream Aida cloth, 40 x 30cm (16 x 12in) • Needle and contrasting sewing thread • Embroidery hoop • Tapestry needle, size 22 • Embroidery ribbon: pastel green, 19m x 1.5mm (21yd x $^{1}/_{16}$in); violet, 6.4m x 1.5mm (7yd x $^{1}/_{16}$in); tea rose and scarlet, 4.6m x 5mm (5yd x $^{3}/_{16}$in); moss green, 6.4m x 1.5mm (7yd x $^{1}/_{16}$in) • Sable double-face satin ribbon, 2m x 1.5mm (2$^{1}/_{4}$yd x $^{1}/_{16}$in) • Strong thread • Mounting (mat) board • Dressmaker's pins

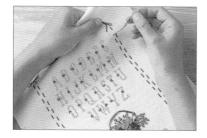

6 Complete the sampler with a simple running stitch around the edge. Use your finger or a large needle to prevent the ribbon from twisting as you stitch. Sew a small ribbon bow in each corner.

7 To mount the sampler on card, remove it from the embroidery hoop and centre the card on the wrong side of the embroidery. Fold over the fabric edges at the top and bottom, securing with pins. Fold over and secure the sides.

8 Using strong thread, sew long lacing stitches between the two side edges of the fabric, tightening as you go. Fasten off the thread firmly before lacing between the top and bottom edges.

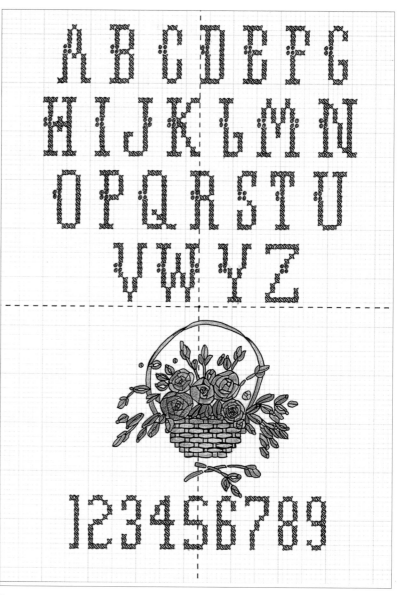

Key

CROSS STITCH: letters and numbers – pastel green
FRENCH KNOTS: decoration on the letters – violet
SPIDER'S WEB ROSES: roses – scarlet and tea rose

LAZY DAISY STITCH: leaves – moss green
STRAIGHT STITCH: rosebuds and border – tea rose and violet

TEMPLATES

CELEBRATION CAKE PP70–1

CHRISTENING PILLOW PP85–6

CLOCHE HAT PP76–7

CLASSIC EVENING PURSE PP67–9

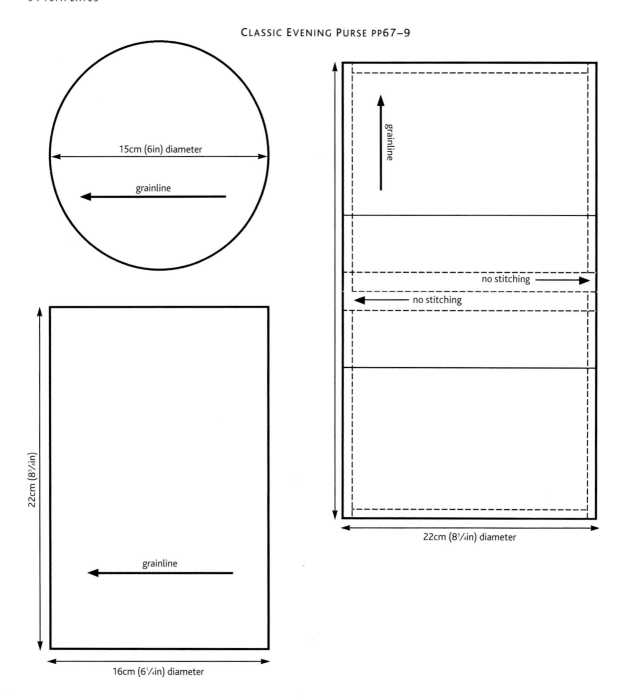

15cm (6in) diameter

grainline

grainline

no stitching

no stitching

22cm (8¾in)

16cm (6¼in) diameter

22cm (8¾in) diameter

SUPPLIERS

United Kingdom

C.M. Offray & Son Ltd
Fir Tree Place
Church Road
Ashford
Middlesex TW15 2PH
Tel: (01784) 247281

Redburn Crafts
Squires Garden Centre
Halliford Road
Upper Halliford
Shepperton
Middlesex TW17 8SG
Tel: (01932) 784121

Doughty Bros Ltd
33 Church Street
Hereford
Herefordshire
Tel: (01432) 352546
www.doughtysonline.co.uk

Fine Fabrics
Magdelene Lane
Taunton
Somerset
TA1 1SE
Tel: (01823) 270986

Clements of Watford
Ground & 1st floor,
Charter Place,
Charter Place Shopping
 Centre,
Watford, WD17 2RX
Tel: (01923) 256006
www.clements.co.uk

Canada and United States

Abbey Arts & Crafts
4118 East Hastings Street
Vancouver, V5C 2J4
Burnaby, B.C.
Tel: (604) 299 5201

Carnmeal Cottage
Tel: +44(0)1326 572901
www.carnmeal.com

JKM Ribbons and Trims
Tel: 800-767-3635
www.jkmribbon.com

Michaels
Numerous craft stores across
 Canada and the USA
Tel: 1-800-642-4235
www.michaels.com

May Arts
Tel: 203-637-8366
http://www.mayarts.com/

Dressew
337 W. Hastings Street
Vancouver,
B.C. V6B 1H6
Tel: (604) 682 6196

Australia

Beutron Australia Ltd.
1 Queen Street
Auburn NSW 2144
Tel: 61(2) 9649 2777
(Contact for list of stockists)

Spotlight
Tel: 1300 305 405
www.spotlight.com.au/

Lincraft
www.lincraft.com.au

ACKNOWLEDGEMENTS

The publishers would like to thank all the people who helped compile this book, particularly the contributors who made the projects: Cheryl Owen, page 32, 34, 46, 51 and 78; Lucinda Ganderton, page 36, 56, 72, 74 and 84; Kelie-Marie Townsend, page 41 and 64; Kate Wilson, page 38; Dorothy Wood, page 44 and 87; Mary Straka, pages 48 and 58; Fiona Barnett, Manic Botanic, page 54 and 81; Judy Clayton, page 60; Sarah King, page 67; Louise Brownlow, page 76; Pat Isaacs, page 90. Also, the institutions who kindly loaned pictures: The Embroiders' Guild, Hampton Court, London, page 8; The Victoria & Albert Museum, London, page 9 and 10, and the Whitchurch Silk Milk, Whitchurch, Hampshire, England, page 11.

The following artists would be pleased to accept commissions for ribbonwork and may be contacted through the publisher: Daphne J. Ashby, Eaton Rise, Eaton by Tarporley, Cheshire CW6 9AF; Jenny Banham, 88 Shaw Drive, Walton-on-Thames, Surrey ET12 2LS; Renata Brink, 13c Lambert Road, London SW2 5BA; Jo Buckley, Tel. 01672 540309; Jenny Chippendale, 4 Glendon Hall, Kettering, Northants NN14 1QE; Steve Cormack, Highland Games, High Street, Dingwall, Ross-shire IV15 9HT; Hikaru Noguchi, Unit 4, Cockpit Workshops, Northington Street, London WC1N; Patricia Tindale, 34 Crescent Grove, London SW4 7AH; Maureen Voisey, 53 Arnesby Road, Lenton Gardens, Nottingham NG7 2E and Pamela Woods, The Pearoom, Heckington, Lincs NG35 9JJ.

They would also like to thank the following companies for lending further items for the photography: The Holding Company, Robert Young Antiques, Joss Graham Oriental Textiles, V. V. Rouleaux, and Paperchase.

INDEX